New Puppy!

Biting? No sleep? Puddles?
How to survive the early weeks and still love your puppy

Beverley Courtney

Books by the author

Essential Skills for a Brilliant Family Dog

Book 1 Calm Down! Step-by-Step to a Calm, Relaxed, and Brilliant Family Dog

Book 2 Leave It! How to teach Amazing Impulse Control to your Brilliant Family Dog

Book 3 Let's Go! Enjoy Companionable Walks with your Brilliant Family Dog

Book 4 Here Boy! Step-by-Step to a Stunning Recall from your Brilliant Family Dog

Essential Skills for your *Growly* but Brilliant Family Dog

Book 1 Why is my Dog so Growly? Teach your fearful, aggressive, or reactive dog confidence through understanding

Book 2 Change for your Growly Dog! Action steps to build confidence in your fearful, aggressive, or reactive dog

Book 3 Calm walks with your Growly Dog. Strategies and techniques for your fearful, aggressive, or reactive dog

Coming soon!
More Skills for a Brilliant Family Dog
Fetch It! Teach your Brilliant Family Dog to catch, fetch, retrieve, find, and bring things back!

www.brilliantfamilydog.com/books

Your free book is waiting for you!

Get the next piece of the puzzle for your dog

Get the first digital book in the series,
Essential Skills for your Brilliant Family Dog
absolutely free here
https://www.brilliantfamilydog.com/freebook-calm-down

Disclaimer

I am not a vet!

In a few places I'll recommend you check something with your vet. Like babies, young puppies can go downhill very fast, so never hesitate to visit your vet if you are at all concerned.

Having said that, puppies will also bounce back fast!

But I'm not a medic of any kind, so any opinions I express are based on my best efforts to study the literature, from personal experience, and from case studies. Not gospel, in other words. In matters of your puppy's health, defer to your vet.

Puppies learn just the same - whether big, small, male, female … I switch from "he" to "she" on a whim.

All the photos in this book are of "real" dogs - either my own, or those of students and readers (with their permission). So the reproduction quality is sometimes not the best. I have chosen the images carefully to illustrate the concepts - so we'll have to put up with some fuzziness.

Contents

Introduction

You're getting a puppy! Such an exciting time!

- It's your first-ever puppy, and you're anxious to get it right.
- Or it's your first-ever puppy and you assume it'll be plain sailing!
- Maybe you've always had a dog - but hey, your lovely pet just died aged 17! and you're a bit rusty on what will happen with your new puppy.
- You could have an older dog in the household and you're concerned at how that will go - or at the other extreme, you think your older dog will train your puppy for you and you won't have to do a thing!

- Maybe all you want is to survive the first few weeks and start nudging your puppy towards being a Brilliant Family Dog.
- Or perhaps you realise that fashions have changed and there's no need to order your dog about or treat it as a lesser being in order to keep control. You want to know what the latest kind methods you've heard about actually are.

You are in the right place!

Help! What have I done?

Whatever your reasons for dipping into this book, you'll be sure to find lots of answers here.

Far and away the great majority of people who visit www.brilliantfamilydog.com and its large store of force-free dog-training articles are new puppy-owners with two questions at the front of their mind:

"I have a new puppy - will I ever sleep again?" and

"Ouch! How can I stop my puppy nipping me/the children/the cat?"

So in this book I address those questions in detail. But I also show you a few other things you need to know to turn your wild puppy into your Brilliant Family Dog! Some things you already know a bit about, and there are others that are a closed book to you. So I'm giving you *all* my secrets to rearing a puppy successfully - without conflict, shouting, dramas, chewed-up phones, spoiled carpets, exhaustion, and wails of "Whose idea was it to get a **** puppy?"

I've reared eleven puppies of my own, I've boarded and homeschooled many more of all kinds and sizes for clients, and I've run small, force-free, Puppy Classes with Puppy Walks for almost ten years. So I kinda know my way around a puppy!

You won't find information on vaccination schedules, what breed of puppy to get, or a lot of what you often find in most puppy books.

This one focusses on the *training* aspect of life with your new pup. There's an extensive section where you'll find links to lots of other puppery - things that I recommend you read, watch, or get - to make life easier with your new family member. And we're not going into detailed training protocols here (though I'll recommend a number to follow on to). This is a book on how to survive the early weeks, and start forming a dog who listens to you and wants to please. Most of them want to please - it's just that they aren't shown how! It's all guesswork for them, and very frustrating all round.

> *You will build a bond with your new dog that is unbreakable*

What do you want?

After all, you didn't get a dog to make your life worse! You need to keep in the front of your mind why you chose to get a puppy in the first place. It's probably somewhere in this list:

- A companion to avoid loneliness
- A playmate for the children
- I grew up with a dog and want my children to enjoy the same
- I want a dog to get me out walking
- I want to try a dog sport
- I want the loyalty and devotion of a dog
- I want to meet other dog-owners
- I ..... [Add your reason here]

These are all laudable aims, but there's one thing you have to remember! Your dog has his own personality, and he'll need to be consulted and given a choice in the matter! He just may hate the thought of competing in a dog sport, or he may be physically unsuited to tramping across the moors. We don't necessarily get the dog (or child) we want - we get the one we're given, and have to enjoy the process of fitting in together. If you've yet to make your choice, check out Chapter 9 without more ado.

What do you expect?

So you may have grand expectations of what you'll do with your new dog-friend. Keep in mind that at the moment he's a baby, soaking up everything like a sponge. It'll be a while before he'll be out on long walks, or be able to behave nicely in a café. Have patience and be prepared to temper your expectations.

You've a long way to go yet, and you'll be finding out just what your chosen dog likes, dislikes, fears, loves … and you'll be making life good for him.

How lenient should I be? How strict?

You may have an idea that you have to control this new little person in your home, lest he try to manipulate you and take over the place. You may have learnt from television programs that you have to be harsh and domineering to get any results.

Do you do that with your new baby? Do you treat your toddler harshly? Your workmates, your partner? Fortunately child-rearing has improved so much that children in a well-adjusted family don't have to suffer the torments and put-downs that children in the past had to endure.

And your puppy doesn't either!

You'll be pleased to know that treating your new pup as a family member, teaching, managing, and just plain loving her, will work much faster than appearing a menacing figure to this little scrap. You will win her heart and soul fast if you show only kindness and wisdom.

"NOOOOOOOO!"

So the first thing to go out of the window is "NO!" and that wagging finger. Also include here NOOOO, NOOO-OO-OOO, tssst and Ah-ah. It's not only unnecessary, it's stressful for both of you, and - more to the point - *it doesn't work.*

Phew. What a relief!

No need ever to say NO to your puppy. Really, I mean that. And no, that doesn't mean mayhem and chaos - you will move together as a team, with clear boundaries and understanding. You will learn how to manage things so that your puppy *cannot* go wrong! You will become *proactive*, not *reactive,* so no firefighting, no clearing up disasters, no coming home to a wrecked kitchen.

Choice

And you'll achieve all this by the simple expedient of giving your dog a CHOICE. Instead of "Do this, do that," you'll be saying - just as you would to another respected family member - "Shall we do this, or would you prefer to do that?" For example, "If I pick up your lead, would you like to come over here to have it clipped on, or would you rather run around like a mad thing, barking, and not get to go out for a walk? It's up to you." "Would you like to go into your crate and wait for your dinner to arrive, or will I put the bowl back in the fridge?"

Of course - as all mothers know! - you weight the choices in your favour. Ideally you don't care which way the puppy chooses, then you don't have an emotional investment in her "getting it right". All that tension will slip from your shoulders as you genuinely give your dog a choice, and watch with interest to see what she chooses.

One of the skills of this method is that when you offer a choice, you have to WAIT for the dog to make her decision. Give her time! We tend to bark commands and not wait to see what our pup thinks. She'll soon find out that the "right" decision earns her something she likes, while the "wrong" decision gets her … nothing. (There's no blame or punishment involved in this - it's truly liberating all round!)

The joy of this method of training is that you never have to *tell* your dog to do anything! Later on, when he knows the words, you can *ask* him. But he learns entirely by doing. It's by doing that we all learn - would you learn to service a car by reading a book or listening to a lecture? No! You learn at your teacher's elbow, getting oil all over you and dropping tools in the wrong places. Just the same way you learnt to bake a cake with your mother, with mistakes and mess and laughter in your enjoyment of the process.

See what wise Confucius said, 2,000 years ago:

> *I hear and I forget.*
> *I see and I remember.*
> *I do and I understand.*

All Day Training

"Do I have to have set training sessions every day? I'm busy …" Of course you are - you're already using all 24 hours in your day. So you may fear that if you don't fit training sessions in, things will start to slide and go wrong. The lunatics will take over the asylum! You'll become one of those dog-owners you hate, with mess and destruction everywhere around you.

Nope! is the answer. If you're working with Choice Training, you'll be using **All Day Training**. Every interaction with your dog is an opportunity for her to learn.

You don't line your children up each morning, and give them a potted 10-minute lecture on what they should or shouldn't do that day! You teach them all the time, whenever you're interacting with them. Your young child asks for the plate of cake in your hand - you wait, staying still, till you get "Please!" then the child gets the cake. This is unconscious child-training, all day training, and you'll do the same with your puppy.

- Every time he looks at you, you can reward him.
- Every time you take him to the garden, he can wait for you to open the door. Gradually he'll learn to sit when you touch the door handle, and when the door is wide open he'll wait to be released - you just start off with him finding that barging ahead doesn't open the door.
- Every time you feed him (more later in the book!) you have the opportunity to teach a little impulse control round something he desperately wants. Your puppy waiting is the same as your child saying Please.
- Every time he goes for a nap in his crate, you can reward him for going straight in quietly.
- And so it goes on, all day. All Day Training. No big time-effort required.

But he does it on purpose!

I am often told how "naughty" a puppy is, because he does something the owners don't like and this causes them to react. (Chasing the puppy to retrieve something he has would be a good example - this actually teaches him to play Keepaway! More in Chapter 8.) In fact, this is good! It shows that he's finding that he can affect outcomes by his actions. It's up to you to teach him what outcomes you'd like, so that he can "make things happen" that you like, and grow in confidence with his good decisions.

And remember a "problem" is only a problem if that's what you call it. Your puppy doesn't see it as a problem - he's just doing stuff. It's your perception that's making it a problem. Interpret it, instead, as "information". Now you've got something you can work with!

Your new mantra!

To help you with this, I have a mantra for you to learn:

> *Reward what you like*
> *Ignore what you don't like*
> *Manage what you can't ignore.*

So, EVERY time your puppy does something you like, you mark it YES! and REWARD him.

Whenever he does something you don't like, you IGNORE it entirely. "I see no puppy."

And in order to avoid situations which you can't ignore (e.g. puppy is chewing your best shoes) you MANAGE things so that he can never get at your shoes (tidy them up!) - or anything else you value.

Once you adopt this method of working with your new pup, you'll find that everything becomes so much easier! No senseless battles, no misunderstandings, no loss of patience for you, no frustration for the dog.

Learn the mantra, pin it up somewhere where the whole household can see it, and check frequently that you're following it, until it becomes second nature.

Your puppy does not understand English (or Polish, or Swahili)

Your puppy does not arrive with human language installed. So repeating things, shouting at him (like at Johnny Foreigner!) is only going to confuse and frighten him. He's not going to suddenly understand.

So while you'll always chat to your little fluffball when you interact with him, teaching him the word for - for instance - SIT, only happens once he's learned to sit.

Baffling? "So how will he sit if I don't tell him?" you may be thinking …

You'll teach your pup how to sit by simply waiting for him to sit and rewarding him. As simple as that! Later on you can add the word "Sit" to describe the action just as his bum is going to the floor. There - you've labelled it. Now he knows what that action is called. This is all done in the context of a game - what's not to love?

You'll find in the Resources section my books which take you through training your dog step-by-step.

Only say it once!

Do you like being nagged? Thought not. Neither does your pup. He'll switch off, just as you would. So when you use a word - any word, be it his name, or sit or whatever you've taught him - you only say it once!

Say it, and ZIP it.

Repeating it endlessly, getting louder and crosser as you go, will not help one bit. If you've taught him the word and rewarded him handsomely for his response then he'll respond automatically as soon as he hears it. If he doesn't respond, either you haven't *actually* taught him that sound, or he's not in a position to respond right now (he's sniffing a fascinating hole in the grass, he's anxious about the dog over there staring at him, he just heard a child scream and doesn't know whether he should flee …)

So say your word and reward your puppy for responding. And if he doesn't respond, check out what is going on which is preventing him - change that, and try again (once!).

You won't actually be using cue-words for some time. (You're never going to use "commands" - how often do you *command* people to do things?) Teach the puppy what you like first, then add the word later. Sounds weird? Don't worry - it'll all become clear!

The Precious Name Game

Here's a starter for you. Your puppy should think her name is precious and never associate that sound with anything bad. You can start teaching this the moment your puppy arrives through the door. Not as a set training session - just part of your All Day Training.

1. For the next five days, whenever you notice your dog, say her name cheerfully - once.

2. As soon as she races to you with tail wagging - or just flickers an eyelid - reward her joyfully with a surprise - attention, fun, game, toy, or a treat.

3. Every third or fourth time she bounces to you, slip your hand softly in her collar, *so she can feel the back of your hand against her neck.* (I always have a loose-but-secure soft collar on new puppies ... just in case.) Don't grip hard. Then release it as you give her reward.

4. Repeat endlessly, all day long.

When you're frustrated or short-tempered, you find your new chairs have acquired decorative toothmarks (where were you?), you need to interrupt your puppy in a hurry - you DON'T use her name. What do you use instead? Absolutely anything you like. From "Puppy!" to "Sausages!", from "Woowoohoo!" to "&**$^**£*!!". Whatever you call, don't call her name.

Dogs are simple creatures. They do what works. And they learn fast.

Simply ensure that you follow the steps above. Focus on it religiously for five days and see where you are.

By the way, often all you need to do to prevent your dog doing something you don't like is to distract her by calling her lovely name. No need to stress yourself out by remonstrating with her. There's no place for Victorian morality in working with your pet! Get the result you want and move on.

Rewards

I've mentioned rewards frequently. What should you use as a reward? Well, what does your puppy find rewarding? It needs to be something that is so good it will stop him in his tracks. For some dogs, like herding dogs or terriers, this will be a toy. But for virtually all dogs, food will hit the spot first!

What kind of food?

Personally, I avoid commercially-produced food altogether. When my children were growing I preferred to feed them with homemade food so I knew what was in it, and could make biscuits, for instance, the right size. The same goes for your dog. You can get great results by taking a couple of minutes to prepare some tasty treats - and it will normally work out much cheaper than shop-bought!

Cheese, sausages, hot dogs - chopped up very small (if you have a toy dog, then chopped up tiny) will work wonders with most dogs. You can have some in a container in the fridge so it's always ready. I'll revisit this later in the book - but for now, make sure you have good stuff to offer!

This won't work for me - my dog is different ...

Yup. It will work for you.

Whether your dog is big or small, male or female, a herder or a guardian, a terrier or a toy, a pedigree or a crossbreed - it will work for you. You've already seen that I refer to your puppy as "he" or "she" as the whim takes me. There's no difference in how they learn.

Get stuck in to the book - and enjoy watching the results!

Day 1

And one last thing - start as you mean to continue! If you never want your dog on the furniture (can't think why not?) then never let him on it. If you never want him to jump up at you, don't accept jumping up without invitation from Day 1 (more about how to do that in Chapter 6). If you want to sleep all night - as you'll see in the very first chapter - start on your puppy's first night with you. Moving the goalposts later on would be puzzling and unfair.

Off you go - to find out how to get your puppy to sleep all night.

In this Introduction we have learnt:

- To shed old-fashioned ideas about "them and us"
- To treat your new puppy as you treat all the others in your family
- That your puppy has to learn first before she can do what you want
- "I like these new people - they understand me."

.

1. Sleeping the night through

You've brought your puppy home. You are excited. The children are bouncing off the walls. And the puppy is … alarmed, confused, and exhausted - however short your journey may have been. So that means he'll sleep like a log, right?

Wrong.

Just a short while ago he was able to cuddle up with a heap of other puppies. Now he seems to be alone, in a strange place with new noises and smells. Will his siblings arrive soon? Will someone from his old home come and take him back? And who are *you*?

He has no idea.

So you're going to need to help him to settle comfortably and get some much-needed sleep.

Picture this: you've done what many people do and decided that your puppy will sleep in the kitchen. It's big enough for her to wander about in and relieve herself on the floor. Trouble is, your cuddly fluffy new puppy turns into a screeching monster as soon as you put your head on your pillow. So you go down to see what's wrong - is she hungry? is she cold? does she need a wee? There's mess all over the floor, her new expensive bed is wet and chewed. By the time you've cleared everything up, both you and your puppy are well and truly awake. The puppy is now refreshed and ready to start the day. But it's half past midnight and you have to be at work tomorrow morning!

This is usually the stage when you fetch the duvet downstairs and try to sleep on the sofa. In no time it's 4 a.m., the puppy is refreshed and you are not.

Next night you eschew your comfy bed and start out on the sofa. You wake up hearing chewing and crunching noises as your puppy discovers the interesting textures of your tv cables. And being awake and mobile, she now needs to relieve herself - this bit of carpet will do …

As you stagger into work on the fourth or fifth day you realise that *This Is Not Working!* That's when I get a phone call. The caller is usually desperate: sleep-deprived, anxious, guilty, worried, their work is being affected, they see no light at the end of this tunnel. Some people actually return the puppy to the breeder at this stage: really!

Maybe you've already had some nights like this and you're getting desperate?

I have to put my hand up and confess that this is how I started out, a very long time ago, with my first puppy Poppy. But I learnt so quickly, that by the time Rupert, puppy no.2, arrived in the family, I'd fashioned a crate out of a tea chest with a weldmesh door which opened and closed with cup hooks! (Crates were not generally available in those days.) And enjoyed a completely new experience of puppy-rearing!

Rafa feels safe in his crate

So where should he sleep?

You may be thinking that curled up on your lap is the best place, or lying by your feet. A lot of people let the puppy sleep wherever he falls. You may have strong ideas that dogs should never go upstairs and the bedroom will be out of bounds.

I'm about to challenge all this and give it to you with both barrels.

So what should you do instead?

I often find people have a crate for their dog, but haven't used it, or they've tried using it but won't shut the door, or it's in the wrong part of the house. They may think it's cruel to confine the puppy to a crate - but I can assure you that the breeder confined the puppies (3? 6? 10 of them?) most of the time!

Most people are comfortable putting their baby in a cot - for their own peace of mind as well as the babe's safety. What's the difference?

The next thing I learn is, "I don't want the dog in the bedroom".

As they are usually at the stage where they are actually paying me to give them a night's sleep, this is particularly shortsighted.

Your puppy is used to snuggling up with those 3, 6, or 10 warm, furry, littermates - suddenly being alone is a loss and causes fear - cue: crying and scrabbling.

The hapless owners have also perhaps been making this common mistake, which one desperate terrier-owner told me about: "I come straight downstairs, knock on the door, and tell her to be quiet."

Your puppy is not barmy - she's able to work out that if she barks and wails long enough, someone will come. Now you've told her she just has to keep going for as long as it takes! You've made things worse!

My own puppies sleep through the night from the day they arrive. They quickly get into a pattern and will be clean and dry by night from anything between 7 and 9 weeks.

Want to know what the secret is?

1. Use a crate

It doesn't need to be the size of a ballroom - only big enough for the puppy to get up, turn around, and lie down again, just as our beds just fit us for sleeping. It's a bed, not a playroom. If you've bought a large one because your pup is a large breed but is currently still tiny, you can either buy a custom crate divider - or simply fill the extra space with cardboard boxes to make a smaller sleeping area. No problem if he chews the boxes. A well-reared puppy will not normally soil his sleeping area (unless very distressed) so this helps with your housetraining program. If you have a whippet, earthdog or other tunnelling breed, provide masses of blankets your pup can burrow into like a hamster, rather than a flat single piece of bedding which will better suit a hot dog like a border collie or a golden retriever. Go for inexpensive bedding - old blankets and the like. Hold off shopping for the expensive stuff till your pup is ready.

If you think you haven't room for a crate (you're mistaken), or don't like the idea of it (you're very mistaken!), you can use a doggy playpen or even baby gates confining the pup to a downstairs toilet or other small space. But really - just get a crate …

2. Shut the crate door

Shut the crate for every nap, every sleep, every meal. Never open the crate door if your dog is hollering "I'm going to get my lawyer if you don't let me out of here!" Only calm and silence will get that door opened. (Genuine distress is something else, and needs attention - you should be able to distinguish between annoyance and distress with ease.) Darken the room and/or partially cover the crate - this makes it a cosy den. For naps, leave the room and shut the door.

3. Put the crate by your bed at night

Your puppy will hear you breathing and moving, sighing and snoozing. If she wakes up anxious, you can just reach a hand out to touch her through the bars so she is reassured she's not alone. You'll hear if she's genuinely agitated and needs a wee. If you don't want your dog to sleep in your bedroom, you can move her out again once a pattern is established and she feels confident in her new home and routine. But don't miss this step because of funny ideas about the dog ruling the household etc. Right now she's a babe, and needs cosseting.

4. Once pup is in crate, there's no talk, no interaction

The crate is a quiet area for s-l-e-e-p-i-n-g. And chewing chew toys, and eating meals. It's not a chatty place.

Imagine the crate is soundproof - both ways!

Whenever you can't be focussing on your puppy, she goes in the crate, perhaps with her meal or a chew toy. This way there is never anything the puppy can do wrong! You will never catch her doing something you don't like! No fights! No arguments! Just pleasure when you return to take her out.

You have now taught your dog to relax and settle anywhere she finds her crate. This is invaluable training for the rest of your lives together! No separation anxiety, no pacing and worrying when you holiday in a new place, no danger of damaging the carpets or cables when visiting friends. When your dog goes into her crate, she lies down and sleeps!

I've given my sleep recipe to anyone who has difficulty settling their new pup, and get responses like these:

"Got a whole night's sleep last night! Thank you!!" *Vizsla puppy 9 weeks*

"Your suggestion about the size of the crate worked wonders! No mess in crate this morning." *Labrador pup 14 weeks*

How long should he sleep?

You'll be pleased to know that your puppy needs to sleep - most of the time. An adult dog needs to sleep 17 hours a day - yes, that's 17 hours a day - for optimum physical and mental health. This is how we can pursue our own busy lives and not feel guilty we're ignoring our dog for chunks of the day. I wouldn't ever leave a puppy longer than 3-4 hours, and you can work up to that.

So if an *adult* dog needs 17 hours sleep a day, how much does my puppy need? More. A lot more.

In the early days, once he's been awake for about an hour, it's time to go back to sleep again. We all know what a fractious, overtired, toddler is like. Your overtired pup will be just the same. Instead of grizzling and screaming and throwing a tantrum like the toddler, he's more likely to go wild and start nipping and grabbing at everything. Reasoning is fruitless, in both cases.

And, in both cases, the answer is simply to deposit the offending, tired, baby in his cot (or crate), turn off the light, and shut the door. Wailing will soon end as sleep takes over. When you go in to wake your babe, he'll be bright and calm and easygoing again. And you'll remember how much you love him.

Crate training

You need to take this crate idea seriously. Training a young pup simply means putting him in there for good things (food, treats, treat-toy, chew, comfort, zzzzz). For an older puppy you may have to work a little harder. You make sure the crate is an attractive place, perhaps half-covered with a cloth to make it a comfy den, and all foody things happen there. You can drop some treats in as you pass, either when the puppy is in there or not, so he learns that checking out the crate will always pay off. You may be surprised how quickly your puppy gets to love his crate! And he'll choose to go there whenever he needs a break.

It's important to have some house rules round the crate - no-one disturbs the puppy when he's there. Not only is the crate "soundproof", it's also wearing Harry Potter's Cloak of Invisibility. It's especially important for children to learn not to pester the puppy. And as every mother knows - you never wake a sleeping child!

Separation Anxiety

Having a safe haven is also going to prevent any hint of Separation Anxiety in your puppy. He'll know that crate = sleep = comfort and safety. Why would he fret? You need to practice brief separations from your puppy from the start, even if for only 3 minutes while you go to the bathroom. Gradually you can extend these periods till you know he is completely content.

Don't know what your dog is doing in the crate when you're not there? Leave a laptop or phone videoing him, or just a sound recorder. Then you'll know. Warning: should be v-e-r-y boring footage.

If you still need convincing, have a watch of the Crate Training video in the Resources section and see what you can do when you have this skill in place!

A typical day for your new puppy

You may have thought - well I just get a puppy and it'll be there to entertain me when I want, then curl up in its basket when not required. He'll fit in with the children and other household pets, and generally be reliable and perfect.

Yes, that will happen.

But it's going to take a lot of management from you to achieve this happy state!

Remember the mantra from the Introduction? Keep this always in your mind. While you are operating within Choice Training, you have to remember that your puppy is not yet equipped to make reliably good choices - he's a baby!

> *Reward what you like*
> *Ignore what you don't like*
> *Manage what you can't ignore.*

So it'll go something like this

7.00 Puppy wakes up

7.01 Puppy taken out to the garden on lead for first wee of the day (See Chapter 7 for full details on Housetraining)

7.05 Puppy eats his breakfast (Meal 1) in his crate while you dress etc

7.15 Puppy taken out on lead for a poo

7.20 Puppy is free to play with his toys in the kitchen while you prepare breakfast for the family. Child/puppy play should always be closely supervised.

Early morning: Pup into crate for first nap while you take kids to school/start work

A couple of hours later: Time for puppy to come out again (wee) and interact with you. Do some of your all day training - the crate door doesn't open till he's waiting patiently, not scrabbling at the door.

Then: More sleep time. Out for a wee and a game, then

Lunchtime: Either Meal 2 in crate, or foodtoy in crate, or handfeed for the Precious Name Game

Early afternoon: If unvaccinated, carry the puppy for an "arm-walk" up and down your street, or to the local shops. If he's doing the walking, keep this walk short (see Chapter 4) and don't expect to get very far.

Play round you while you work/prepare evening meal

As soon as he looks droopy, back into crate for another sleep, especially if children are due home. He sleeps while you collect the children/go shopping/work.

Meal 3 in crate, perhaps while children are eating and still excited

Play - actively supervised if children are involved.

Early evening: Meal 4, wee, quiet time in Living Room with you and his toys.

Bed

You see? Mostly sleep!

Remember too that you're going to start this schedule from Day 1 of your puppy's life with you.

TROUBLESHOOTING

Q My 9-week-old puppy needs to go out for a pee 3-4 times a night. I expected this, but I'm getting exhausted!

A At this age she's likely to need to go out during the night. But she doesn't need to go out 3-4 times! Unless there's a physical reason, in which case have a Vet check. If she's in a crate in your room you'll hear her getting restless and can take her out. Some of my dogs have been clean and dry by night from the moment they arrive, bigger dogs may be 9-10 weeks before that happens. Keep it all very low-key, little interaction, back to bed. Remember that what you expect is often what you get!

Q I tried the first night leaving my puppy loose - never again! Tonight she'll be in her crate. But will she keep waking up the same amount?

A Like dogs, we have a sleep cycle of an hour and a half or so - we surface and then go back to sleep. This is where the crate scores. If the puppy is loose, she'll wake, get up, wander about, need a pee, suddenly realise she's alone - cry, etc. If she stirs in her sleep in her crate, she'll just turn over, like we do, and go back to sleep again.

Q My 16-week-old pup is always happy to go in the crate and sleeps all night. It's just when we leave that she gets worked up and may wet her bed. Is this Separation Anxiety?

A Crate: this needs to be just big enough for your puppy to get up, turn round and lie down again. If it's bigger than that, either use a custom divider or put in some cardboard boxes to shrink the space down to just her sleeping area. A pup is reluctant to soil the bed. No water in the crate.

Give her a food-toy as you leave which she *only* gets in the crate. It can be a kong with paté or peanut butter (xylitol-free) smeared around inside. By the time she's cleaned this out she should be tired and ready to sleep and not have noticed you going. You can freeze some food-toys ready.

You're right, it's the moment of departure which causes the distress. Once she's over this she can settle. Practice departures when you're not actually going anywhere, even staying in the house. Ignore any noise from the crate. Remember it's soundproof - both ways!

Q My kids are so excited, they're creeping down in the night to wake the puppy!

A Aw, bless them! Another great reason to have the crate in your room ... Everyone will do better tomorrow with their full complement of sleep.

Q I get my new puppy today! How can I get her to sleep tonight?

A Just follow all the guidance in this chapter. And have a look at this comment about a new 7-week-old puppy:

> "Since we just got her yesterday, there wasn't much time to introduce the crate to her prior to bedtime. I had the crate next to our bed and made it such that the divider gave her just enough room. She did whine a few times at night, but we waited until she stopped before we took her out to toilet. There were times I'd put my finger in the crate to stroke her and she'd fall back asleep."

Perfect! That's how it's done!

In this chapter we have learnt:

- Where your puppy should sleep
- How long he should sleep (critical!)
- A typical day for a new pup
- "Zzzzzz …"

2. Biting - ouch!

Indie and Waffle sharing clothes pegs

This is the second most popular question I receive! It's common for someone to say, "I expected the puppy to nip, but he's now 4/6/10 months old and it hurts!"

Sadly this reader has failed to lay some simple ground rules with their pup - again, from Day 1 of your puppy's life with you - which would have stopped this unwanted biting within a few days of his arrival.

Parents are often distressed too, when the new puppy the children so wanted seems to be intent on ripping them to shreds ... to the extent they don't want to play with her any more!

Why the nipping?

Babies explore the world with their mouths, puppies do the same. The only difference is that babies have gums, while puppies have needles!

Everyone seems to expect a bit of puppy nipping when they get a puppy. According to my oft-quoted maxim that "What you expect is what you get", this can be a self-fulfilling prophecy.

I can also add that "What you *accept* is what you get"!

And I find many new puppy-owners accept a level of savagery from their puppy which astonishes me. I'm often shown arms covered with scratches, scabs and nasty bruises. And I'm here to tell you that this is totally unacceptable!

I can honestly say that my own puppies learn that dogs' teeth never touch human skin - very, very fast. In a few days. And they will never have been yelled at or told off.

Help! My puppy thinks my toddler is another puppy!

This is a frequent cry from first-time puppy-owners - or first-time-since-they-had-children puppy-owners. The perfect family home - full of joy and laughter - that they anticipated when they brought a puppy into their midst is crumbling about their ears. They start to regard the puppy as the enemy, instead of a welcome friend. He's a nuisance, and has to be kept under increasing control. This is not a good way to start any relationship.

When the puppy is very new and very tiny and wants to play roly-poly with their small child, this may elicit approving nods and smiles from the parents. But they soon learn that the puppy develops at a much faster rate than their baby, and is also armed with sharp claws, sharp teeth, and an astonishing ability to jump high! It's only when their puppy hits teen-weeks (about fourteen weeks and up) and they realise these games are getting out of hand - when their toddler's happy gurgles turn to wails of pain and fear - that they decide *Something Needs To Be Done*. And by now it's all become a well-established habit.

The answer is simple, but multi-faceted. There's a lot going on here.

The right age to get your puppy

To start off we need to go back a little in time. The ideal age to get a puppy is eight weeks. There are many reasons for this, but for this chapter we'll focus on how this lowers the chances of the puppy nipping and biting us. By six weeks or so, the bitch has usually had enough of her pups and will often be separated from them for most of the time. But this doesn't mean they're not learning!

The time in the litter from six to eight weeks of age is prime socialising time. They find out what works with their littermates and what doesn't. Puppies have a thick fur coat, so the immature jaw control doesn't do them any damage. But a pup will soon tell his brother if the play gets too rough, and the biting too hard. A puppy who is bullying his littermates will become Billy-no-mates until he learns to tone down his enthusiasm. He'll learn this quickly - and what he's learning is called **Bite Inhibition**. He can use his mouth with exquisite control - he can grip without biting, touch without ripping, pull without shredding.

So eight weeks is best. If you're fobbed off with a puppy of 6 weeks, this is purely to suit the "breeder" * - the last two weeks is the most active time for a litter of pups, and the time of most work for the bitch's owner, and if he leaves the nest early your puppy will have missed out on this valuable period of learning with his littermates. And if you get your pup at 10 weeks or older, habits will be established which don't include care of human skin.

* Why "breeder" in inverted commas? Because I would only give that title to someone who knows what they're doing, who plans carefully for the mother and puppies' health, and who only has a litter to improve their breed. This totally excludes puppy farms, puppy mills, backyard breeders, and possibly the woman down the street whose bitch was "caught". Not got your puppy yet? For more detail on how to choose a breeder then choose your puppy, see Chapter 8 Choosing a Puppy

Occasionally you'll find a "singleton" - a puppy in a litter of one. No littermates to teach him Bite Inhibition. In this case you have to do it yourself!

When you play with your new puppy and he bites too hard on your fingers, you can give a single yelp and withdraw yourself from play for a few moments. This is exactly what any littermates would have done. (No NOOOOs.) He'll soon learn what level of bite is acceptable.

I have to laugh when I see someone get nipped, then bend over the puppy staring, wagging a finger. The puppy eyes the finger, "gets the message" and grabs it!

As we saw in Chapter 1, once he arrives with you, your puppy should have a safe den (a crate is ideal) where he can retire or be taken when tired, and which is totally out of bounds to children and other animals.

Games

Teach the puppy which games or parts of games are acceptable. It's quite possible for a dog to understand that they may chase something but not bring it down. Think Border Collie - these amazing dogs can replicate their instinctive hunting patterns by stalking, flanking, driving and chasing sheep, but they never close in for the kill. Friendly chase games in the garden are great for using up lots of energy from both the owner or child, and the dog. A very mouthy puppy can be encouraged to carry a soft toy in his mouth, so there's no danger of grabbing. Teach your children to play statues and freeze the moment the pup gets over-excited and tries to grab a trouser-leg or sleeve. Once the "prey" is still, the hunt is over, and pup will let go - especially if a moving toy is whizzed past his nose for him to focus his chasing on. It goes without saying - but I'll say it anyway - that such games must always be very closely supervised.

No-one should ever play with the puppy without a soft toy in their hand.

I'll say that again: No-one should ever play with the puppy without a soft toy in their hand.

The pup should always be encouraged to play with the toy, down at floor level - not leaping up to grab it from the hand. Get into the habit of always having a knotted sock or small fluffy toy in your pocket - or at least have them around the room so you can always reach out and grab one. When he releases the toy you reward him with another quick game, or a treat if playtime is over. Teeth on skin causes the game to stop for a moment for all sides to calm down, regroup, and remember the rules. Then the game can resume. Give him a choice - play with the toy and we carry on, play with my trousers or fingers and we stop.

If the puppy has gone wild and over the top, this is a sure sign that he's tired and is no longer able to make rational decisions: an hour or two's napping in his crate will restore equilibrium. And if your toddler is also screeching and squawking, it looks like you're going to get a peaceful couple of hours while they both have a nap!

> *"We did have a few issues with playbiting but we have started putting Daisy in her pen for a chill-out and this has worked really well in the last couple of days. I think she was just overtired!"*

Tug

Tug is the Best Game Ever - for teaching impulse control, interactive play, good play habits, letting go, and - of course - no mouthing or biting.

Practice makes perfect! The more you play controlled tug games with your puppy, the better he'll get at instantly releasing the toy when you ask and waiting patiently for the game to start again. To start with, just hold a tasty treat to his nostrils and wait - without pulling the toy at all - for him to let go, even if it's reluctantly. He'll learn that the opportunity to play is dependent on demonstrating impulse control.

It doesn't matter what breed or type your puppy is. Don't believe the old wives' tales about playing tug making them vicious. This is nonsense. All dogs have the same instinctive drives - to locate prey, stalk it, chase it, catch it, and kill it. Some breeds have been designed to stop somewhere in that sequence - the Border Collie stops before catching, the gundog stops before killing - and others are meant to follow the whole sequence. You put a terrier in the barn to get rid of the rats.

But just because you're simulating the "catch" part of the sequence, with the prey animal (your teddy bear) trying to escape and the dog desperately holding on to his dinner, doesn't mean that your dog will not be able to control his bite!

If you give me an ice cream, I know to lick it. If you offer me a biscuit I know to bite it. I don't have to stop and think about this! And neither does your pup. In the video linked in the Resources section, you'll see Lacy holding the tug gently in her mouth, then tugging mercilessly, prior to picking up the phone for me - gently. You can help your dog to use his mouth in different ways.

Nine Rules for Playing Tug

1. *It's your toy.* You allow your dog to play with it when you want, and only if he keeps to the rules. Because it's never left on the floor with the other toys, and the only time your dog gets to play with the tug is with you on the end, it becomes a very high-value toy.

2. You are harnessing a very strong *instinctive drive* in your dog - to stalk, chase, pounce, capture, shake and kill his prey - and turning it to your advantage instead of trying to work against it.

3. When playing, always keep the *tuggie low on the floor* - this is to prevent your pup jumping and injuring himself, it also keeps the teeth pointing downwards and he's less likely to grab your hand or sleeve.

4. Start by snaking the tuggie around on the floor, *like a rabbit -* stop, twitch whiskers, run - this is what stimulates the chase instinct and is the signal to play. You never let go of the tug.

5. Encourage him to *grip tight on the tug* - have a great game, but don't be too rough or hurt his teeth. Growling is part of the game. Pull steadily only with the same force he is using. Don't shake or rattle him about.

6. *If his teeth touch your hand* or sleeve, your dog will be aware, so shriek once to interrupt him, put tug behind your back, and wait for calm before offering it again. He should now be much more careful. If he's over the top, put it away till later.

7. When you're ready, *first relax your pull* so the tuggie goes limp (animal now dead) as you hold a treat to your dog's nose. As he lets go to eat the treat, put the tuggie behind your back (don't take it past your face!). The reward for letting go? Your dog gets to play again!

8. Bring the tug out from behind your back, hold it out above him and twitch it and *tease him a little* with it. If he tries to leap and grab it, it goes straight behind your back (never past your face). Repeat till he shows that he wants it but is not jumping or grabbing, then immediately whack it to the floor - game on! The split-second he doesn't jump, he gets the game again.

9. As you both become more expert at this game - which should become your dog's top favourite - you can use the cue "Geddit" as you whack the tuggie to the ground, and "Give" as your empty hand approaches his nose.

Good toys for play!

Children and puppies

You got a puppy for your family because you wanted your children to enjoy their childhood with a dependable friend - perhaps as you did when you were a child. But don't toss natural safeguards out of the window!

Give the puppy a fighting chance - never leave any child alone with any dog, not even for a moment. If you have to leave the room, take one of them with you.

Supervision should be active, not simply a distracted presence in the same house. When puppy and child are both loose at the same time, this should be the parent's focus. Clever manipulation of sleep and mealtimes may minimise these times a lot, and allow you to devote all attention to either the child or the puppy (or, occasionally, yourself!). You have to be sure that you spend time on your puppy and not just drop him into the mix as a tagalong: this puppy is not going to train himself!

Just before you head for the nearest keyboard to tell me this was how your grandparents grew up, running wild with puppies, I'll put in that things have changed a lot since then. In many ways lifestyles and puppies are different. Let's start from where we are now.

Both child and pup need to learn manners and boundaries. In neither case is this done by shouting, saying NO, or scolding. Showing and encouraging is the way to go.

In time your adult dog will be your growing children's very best friend. But while he's still a baby your puppy needs a lot of guidance and management - and protection. You can't expect to toss the puppy into the family and let him sink or swim. You were already busy every moment of the day before your puppy arrived. So you're going to need to carve out some time for playing with him and teaching him what he can do to please you, while still having a whale of a time being a dog.

If you haven't been near a dog training school for years, you'll be glad to know that the best and most forward-looking have changed beyond recognition! The very best schools now teach mostly through games, and they are entirely force-free. You should feel that you and your children are welcome at the class, and you should also feel confident that the trainer could "train" your toddler in the same way as they show you how to train your puppy, without you being concerned for your child. No doubt you teach your toddler with kindness and patience? There's no need to act differently with your puppy - who's merely another toddler in your family, and who has to be managed, and learn to follow the rules, just the same as the other children.

You simply have to show him how.

An unbreakable bond is growing between this child and her puppy

TROUBLESHOOTING

Q I can't get down the stairs in the morning without my puppy hanging on to my dressing gown.

A Two things here: 1. Have your puppy contained in some way overnight so that you can be ready for when he emerges. And 2. He's grabbing the moving target! Your dressing gown flapping round your ankles is a bunny or rat to him. So stand still, grab the toy from your pocket (yes, even your dressing gown pocket should have a toy!) and engage him with something he's allowed to grab and pull.

Q. My puppy doesn't seem to play with toys at all - is there something wrong?

A. Nope! Some pups are avid chewers and grabbers, some not so much. This is a great opportunity for you to teach a "hold" and retrieve from scratch - just the way you want it. I once had a delightful black and tan Border Collie called Dodger who had had a bit of a neglected childhood before he came to me. He didn't understand toys at all. So along with teaching him to play with toys, I taught him a Competition Obedience retrieve from the start. Dodger always got full marks for his competition retrieve: no pouncing, snatching, chomping, dropping … and certainly no teeth on skin! You can teach your puppy to enjoy toy games with you. First find out what she likes - chase, pounce, grab, pull, worry … then that's the game you play together. This will gradually assume the Tug Rules and turn into a keen retrieve.

Q. I've been told that if my puppy plays tug he'll never be any good as a gundog.

A. I do so love exploding myths! Yep, this is another of those old wives' tales that gets passed down. People like to control things, and creatures. And control tends to mean shutting down opportunity. What could be sillier than preventing a dog learning to play with you - the most important person in his world? Check out that video (Resources Section) which shows you all the different ways a dog can "handle" an article in his mouth. As an award-winning sheepdog-trial shepherd once said to me, "All my best dogs have loved playing football with the kids." If you can make work into play, life becomes so much more fun!

Q We start off well with Tug, then she gets over-excited and leaps up to grab my hand. I'm afraid she'll get my face. She's an 18-week-old terrier.

A. Breed is not terribly important - all dogs can learn to play within the rules, and then it becomes much more fun. Imagine trying to play tennis with someone who stayed on the same side of the net as you - or just hit all the balls out over the fence? All our games have rules. Even young children playing will dictate the rules: "You have to stand on one leg," "You're not allowed to touch the wall," and the like. So this is a time for your Mantra! *Reward* (by playing more tug or giving attention), *Ignore* (by standing stock still and not interacting), *Manage* (by showing that there's no play if she's mad and jumping - into the crate for a short rest, then offer the toy again for a very short session. If she's too mad you may need to gently take her by the collar into the crate, and definitely give her a chewtoy to engage her mouth).

Q I flap the toy in his face and he just looks the other way.

A Rabbits don't jump into dog's mouths! They scurry and freeze, twitch their whiskers, bob away … This is the action you need to simulate with your toy. Always keep it low and snake it along the ground. Try this for a few seconds then put the toy away. Don't stand right over him - give him space. A toy on a rope is ideal for this. Repeat tiny sessions till he shows interest and starts to look alert, follow and pounce. Stamping on the toy may be the first sign of engagement. Keep games very very short till he's got it.

In this chapter we learnt:

- Why some puppies bite everything
- How the puppy's early weeks affect this
- How to teach bite inhibition and the importance of play
- "Whoopee - I get to do what I love best!"

3. Socialisation

Nose-to-nose greetings should be three seconds long at most

You may have heard that Socialisation is very important for your puppy. That's excellent - you're right! But you need to know what exactly socialisation is, *what socialisation isn't,* when it takes place, where, and how. If you get it wrong you don't get a second chance! So it's essential to know what you're doing from the start. It's true that occasionally a puppy comes through entirely the wrong upbringing - and turns into a super pet! But many more present all kinds of behaviour problems as a result. Do you really want to play Russian Roulette with your pet's future?

Is it really necessary?

Socialisation is the single most important thing you should be doing with your new puppy. You've got the rest of your life to teach sits and downs and all the rest, but the construction of the dog's brain means that socialisation is what you have to focus on *right now*.

There's a growing understanding of the importance of socialisation for your puppy. This is a good step forward, but it has also brought a lot of misunderstanding with it! So let's get this cleared up so you know what you're at.

First - what Socialisation is!

Socialisation, Habituation, and Familiarisation - to give it its full title - means that everything you want your dog to cope with in her life is experienced in her first few weeks. (That's why we're in a hurry!) The dog's brain is made so that everything the puppy experiences between the ages of 3 weeks and about 16 weeks is absorbed, processed and given the ok. Anything your puppy comes across after 16 weeks may be worrying, alarming, or frightening.

If you've just got your puppy and he's already hit 16 weeks, you've missed the boat. But don't panic! See "Older Puppies" below.

While we need to introduce these things early on - within that narrow window of time - we need to keep exposing the dog to these same things as she grows. Even if you were taken everywhere as a baby, but then kept at home till you were 12 years old, you'd have a lot of anxieties about the outside world and other people! A simple walk to the shops could be a nightmare.

So you need to keep taking your dog out and about with you so that she can continue to have good experiences round new things.

> *The more novelty your puppy experiences, the better she will accept novelty in the future.*

And *good* experiences is what they must be! If your puppy is happy and curious, then this is a good experience. If she's anxious or shying away, then it's not - so take her back a bit and let her look from further away. The right distance is critical to how she views the encounter.

Remember that everything is new for your puppy - she's only been on the planet a matter of weeks! What *you* take for granted is weird for her. If your puppy is afraid or pulling away, have endless patience. She'll move forward when she's ready. This isn't about "strong wills" or "stubbornness" - it's just fear.

You never get this time again. Once it's gone, it's gone. So you must move correct and appropriate socialisation to the front of your mind and focus on that for now. You have the rest of your life to teach all the other stuff. This thing has a sell-by date stamped on it!

On no account delay taking your puppy out till his vaccination schedule is complete. You will lose critical time. There's no need to expose him to infection - you can carry him, or put him in a pushchair if he's massive and too heavy for you! Car drives are great. He can meet other vaccinated dogs, so can visit your friends and family. Treat him as you would a new baby - just be sensible!

Here are some activities you want to be sure to include - daily, or almost daily:

- Give your puppy good new experiences in a controlled way - people, children, children on scooters, people with hats, dogs, black dogs, big dogs, cats, cows, sheep, tractors, noisy dogs, motorbikes, cars, people shouting, plastic sacks, hot air balloons, towns, shops, countryside, schools, fairs, horses, bikes, trains, teenagers, sirens, wobbly chairs, grass, gravel, slippery floors, pond, squeaky pram wheels - the list is endless.

- Let her find the world is a good place. If she freezes and doesn't want to move forward - stay still and wait with her. Give her a choice in her explorations.

- Allow her to explore - in safety. So you may be carrying her till she's completed her jabs.

- She needs to see lots of dogs and people and children of all shapes, colours, ages, and sizes - but she doesn't necessarily need to *meet* them - yet.

- Playing with dogs: this should be equal play - I chase you, you chase me; I stand over you, you stand over me, we play hippo jaws without using our teeth. If one pup is calling all the shots, stop the interaction immediately and find a more suitable playmate.

- A first-rate force-free Puppy Class will give you lots of tools and experience, though it won't do the socialising for you! Just because there are a few other puppies there doesn't mean your puppy is benefitting from the experience.

Socialisation is what *you* have to do during the remaining 167 hours of each week. It's a commonly-accepted myth that it's necessary to attend classes for the purpose of socialisation. It's absolutely not! Puppy Play in class is fraught with dangers - you need a well-qualified and highly-experienced class tutor to be able to handle it right. Most times this is not the case.

Processing this information

Your puppy needs sleep after any new experiences to process all this new information. As he's sleeping every couple of hours anyway, this is easy to arrange.

What socialisation is not (Myths exploded)

For a start let's get rid of some of the misconceptions. As I said above, "Socialisation" is a blanket term used to describe the process of Socialisation, Habituation, and Familiarisation that the puppy goes through from 3 weeks to about 14-16 weeks of age. This time flies by very fast! So you need to have this always in mind from the minute your puppy arrives with you - you haven't got very long at all.

Socialisation is not only about other dogs. It includes everything in our world.

Here are some examples of what you *don't* want to be doing. Actually, they're all things people will *tell* you to do - even some people you think should know! But here is the official low-down:

- Don't push your puppy towards strange dogs in the hope that it'll go well
- Don't attend a poorly-run puppy party which is just a free-for-all

- Never pass your puppy from person to person (imagine how terrifying that could be for your tiny pup!)
- Don't risk a bad experience by not knowing the other dog's reaction to puppies (not all people like children, not all dogs like puppies). Just say no thanks and move on. The wellbeing of your puppy is your chief concern. This is no time for appearing to be a happy-go-lucky earth-mother and letting other people dictate.
- Don't allow your pup to be swamped by cooing admirers and excited children
- Don't overwhelm your puppy - taking her to a country fair for the day, for instance - this could come under the heading of *flooding* which has the potential to make your puppy "shut down", so she gives up and appears ok but is, in fact, far from it! It's a form of learned helplessness seen tragically in long-term prisoners, beaten children, and abused dogs in those pernicious puppy farms.
- Never allow your dog to jump up all over strange dogs expecting a good outcome

Puppy play

Puppy play should always be closely supervised

Puppies playing together is what people tend to picture - and expect - when they think of socialisation. But as you've seen, it's not! It may be a small part of socialisation, but it's far more important that your puppy can learn to be in the presence of other dogs without having to leap all over them.

Getting your puppy to give you some focus in the presence of other puppies is far more valuable than uncontrolled play!

Puppy play should *always* be supervised. If there's an organised group of puppies, then the organiser should be trained and skilled in understanding dog body language and puppy behaviour. A gang of puppies in a small space is not a safe prospect. Twos and threes work much better, and in general avoids the possibility of the playground bully. You need plenty of space. Never be afraid to jump in and rescue your puppy if she's getting overwhelmed.

Small dogs have to get used to big dogs, and big dogs have to learn how to greet smaller ones. See Tigger learning here!

Friendly pup Tigger is too boisterous for shy Django

That's better, Tigger!

This is the Puppy Play you should look for

Here is a splendid sequence of two puppies of similar age and build demonstrating appropriate, equal, play. Note all the turntaking.

What about older puppies?

You cannot "socialise" an older dog. This is something that can only happen in the dog's brain up to the age of 15-16 weeks. This is one of the reasons it's so important to get your puppy at 8 weeks of age! So if your puppy is over 16 weeks or so when you got him, you have to follow a slightly different process.

What you *can* do is get him out and about, having new experiences, and enjoying them! If he's not enjoying - for instance another dog walking towards him - then about turn and withdraw to a safe distance where he can observe the dog passing while you pop treats into his mouth. The distance will vary, but could be at least 50 yards. Once the dog has passed you can stop with the treat-popping. You're aiming to change your dog's emotional response to the thing he fears. Many dogs who have missed out on proper and timely socialisation become "reactive" as they mature, and bark at every dog they see.

If you're having problems with your dog reacting to other dogs or people, or having a generalised anxiety about everything outside the house, then check out the Resources section for help for your Growly Dog - there's loads there to get you started on making a change without upsetting your fearful dog. And the sooner you start, the better - while your puppy's brain is still developing and forming opinions.

My puppy will be a playmate for my older dog!

This may work … or it may not, without great care. Keep in mind that your older dog didn't choose to get a puppy - *you* did! You can't just toss a new puppy in with older resident dogs and hope it will go well.

So to maintain harmony in the home, you need to protect your older dog from endless puppy attention. A general rule would be a maximum of twenty minutes a day of free play, which would be closely supervised, in five-minute bursts. The puppy is not free to pester people, children, or other household residents, whenever he feels like it. This is important learning for him.

Protect older dogs, cats, and small children from too much attention. How much is too much? That depends on the victim. When they say it's enough, it's enough.

If you have a multi-dog household, your crate will be invaluable! You want to ensure your older dogs are not annoyed, and that the new puppy doesn't have any bad experiences. So monitor all interaction, always.

You will need to devote a lot of 1-1 time to your new puppy - solo walks are essential. And if your older dog is reactive or fearful when out, be sure never to take the two out together. Reactivity is highly catching! See Resources for more on this.

My 7-year-old Border Collie Rollo was protected from Coco Poodlepup till he was a few months old, then they were closely supervised when together. They didn't get to be free together till Coco was around 7 or 8 months old.

The playpen, opened up and zigzagged across the room as a divider was perfect. Careful introductions meant that they rub along fine now. Coco never attempts to initiate play with Rollo as he knows that would not be welcome - though very occasionally Rollo will start a short game with Coco.

15 week-old Coco is permitted to play with 8 year-old Rollo

Keeping dog and puppy apart during the critical learning period also meant that Coco now responds to me rather than his doggy housemates. Time and again I see where people have made the big mistake of letting the dog and puppy entertain themselves together all day long, with little owner input. By the time the younger dog is about a year old, he is interested only in what the other dog does. You're making a rod for your training back if you do this!

Don't be the owner who shook her head sadly at her two misbehaving young dogs and said, "I wish I'd listened to you a year ago ..."

A word about children

While you'll be teaching your own children how to approach dogs - and whether they want to be approached or not - you must watch out for other children who may think your puppy is a plaything provided for their pleasure, instead of a living sentient being who has her own likes, dislikes, and opinions!

If children want to meet your puppy, they have to do it one at a time, from in front, and without screaming and waving their arms around. Banging the pup on the head or back (why do people do this?) is going to give the puppy a bad association with children. Never let your puppy be swamped by a gaggle of shrieking children!

If you play it carefully for the first number of weeks, your dog will become your children's beloved companion - giving them the childhood you want, with outdoor games and adventures, consideration for others, learning how to learn and how to teach. Perhaps your own happy doggy childhood experiences are what drove you to get a dog for your family now. Just take the first few weeks slow and gentle, and keep in mind your puppy's individual personality.

There are some splendid recommended sources of information on Children and Puppies in the Resources section.

Handling

Five Second Rule

And this leads on to handling and touching. Handling is something your pup needs to be acclimatised to, just like everything else in her life. A good move is to employ the Five Second Rule. If your puppy solicits attention from you, you can handle and fuss her for the count of five. Then you detach and take your attention away. Your pup will probably do one of two things: nuzzle you for more attention (she gets another five seconds), or give a shake and walk away (let her go).

You can adapt this - for children it may only be three seconds. For strangers it may be two seconds … or no seconds at all if your puppy doesn't welcome it. You can tell by whether or not she moves forward to the person for attention. Always give your dog a choice.

Grooming

Each day a little grooming should feature in your interactions with your puppy. Some dogs love this, some .. well, they just don't. So you may - starting with the shoulders and upper back - go *stroke, stroke, treat, brush, treat, stroke, brush, treat, finish.* You'll gradually add more brushing to the mix, and more body locations. You can even reward your puppy for just looking at the brush, or sniffing it. Associate good things (treats) with the brush and this will gradually extend to grooming and claw-clipping. Always check ears, paws, and anus, for mats, mess, and foreign bodies.

Don't grab your puppy and spin her on her back to reach some parts! How would you like this if your hairdresser did it to you? This can all be done slowly, a little at a time, with her permission. She won't need real, deep, brushing for many months. The adult coat "guard-hairs" will slowly emerge through the puppy fluff which becomes the insulating "vest". They'll start along her back looking shiny and sleek.

Fluffy pups will need to be shorn and/or shaven every 6 weeks or so. Best to get the gear and do it yourself, a little at a time. It honestly is not hard! Here's Coco Poodle with a fresh clip. He hops up onto the table as soon as he sees the clippers brought out. He was first shaven at 7 weeks old, so is now a seasoned pro.

Acclimatise your pup to the nail clippers in the same way, with a treat for each interaction. *See clippers - treat, sniff clippers - treat, clippers touch foot - treat, clippers touch claw - treat, finish.* This may need to happen over a number of very brief sessions. Next time, repeat the sequence and fiddle about with the claws a bit with your fingers before you ever get to clip.

If your puppy has black claws, have a look at a dog who has clear claws - then you can see exactly where the quick grows to. That's the red bit that you don't want to cut. Frequent clipping of a small amount of claw is far better than leaving it for ages then having a load to chop off.

There's no law that says all the puppy's claws should be trimmed at once! One claw a night may be plenty. Same goes for brushing. Gradually spread over the whole body. You have plenty of time before the adult coat comes in, and she won't be moulting for many months yet. Remember to give her a choice in her care. If you pick up the brush and she hightails it to her crate, then you have work to do! Go back to slow acclimatisation, with plenty of treats.

The slower you go, the sooner you'll get there.

TROUBLESHOOTING

Q I've been told I should take my puppy to the dog park as soon as I can, and just let the dogs sort it out themselves.

A Nooooo! Would you toss your baby into a playschool without any supervision or guidance? I think not! Socialisation is not about going into the fray with a load of strange dogs. Socialisation is about giving your puppy positive experiences about everything she comes across. If you foresee a poor outcome, get your puppy outa there.

Q My vet says I mustn't take my puppy out till several weeks after his last injection. Will he miss out?

A Check that your vet isn't referring to a localised outbreak of disease. As long as this is ok, start carrying your pup out now. Just be careful where you put him down on the ground, and which dogs he meets. But whatever you do, don't miss the window up to 15 weeks of age! You can never get this time back again.

Q My older dog spends a lot of time with the new puppy. This should do, shouldn't it?

A Nope. It's great that they get on well, but your puppy isn't learning anything about other dogs (small dogs, big dogs, black dogs, prick-eared dogs, horses, buses, schoolchildren, planes, noisy workmen …). She needs lots of solo time with you, out and about, exploring.

Q I'm worried that my puppy's first experience of the vets will include being stabbed by a needle. Will this put her off vets for life?

A This is such a good question! Like everything else, "gradual, happy introduction" is the way you want to go. So carry your pup in to your vets when the waiting room is empty, chat with the vet nurse, dish out treats, and leave. I regularly visit my vets - even with my adult dogs - for no reason, just to weigh the dog, say hallo, let them have a sniff round, and go.

Q So socialisation is *not* about playing with other dogs? I always thought it was.

A You and many others! Socialisation is about building your dog's confidence while carefully exposing him to everything he's likely to meet in his life. It's easy to miss things. If, for instance, you like to go on sailing holidays in the summer and you have a winter puppy, then you must work on boats and water being good things *in the first few weeks you have her*. You'd need to have something that will simulate a life-jacket, and perhaps a paddling pool. Even the bath will help! Put a little water in, so part of the bath is still dry, sprinkle in some kibble and toys, and plonk your new puppy in there while you get washed. Gradually add more water over the weeks as her confidence and enjoyment grows.

In this chapter we have learnt about:

- What, where, and how to socialise
- Common socialisation myths
- Socialisation with other dogs
- Touch and grooming
- "I'm happy with new things"

4. Exercise

How much exercise?

You may have got your new puppy with a view to endless games in the garden with the kids, or perhaps tramping over hill and dale for hours at a time. And you're keen to get started!

But remember, your pup is still a baby right now, and you need to keep a careful eye on his levels of exercise in order to keep his joints and bones safe. So how long should you exercise your pup for?

The English Kennel Club says: "A good rule of thumb is a ratio of five minutes' exercise per month of age (up to twice a day) until the puppy is fully grown, i.e. 15 minutes (up to twice a day) when three months old, 20 minutes when four months old."

But this is just a guide! If you have a heavy, giant, slow-maturing, breed you'll be limiting exercise for a long time. A small terrier, however, may be ready to let rip at 9 months or so.

What sort of exercise?

While exercise is vital for building a strong exploring mind as well as a strong skeleton, be aware of what type of exercise you are encouraging.

Keep in mind also the terrain:

- Pavement - very short walks (that's VERY short - maybe 30 yards for a pup under 3 months).
- Deep sand, also short walk.
- Rocks and gravel, snow, ice - short walk only (sliding on slippery surfaces can be particularly damaging for a puppy).
- Really only let your dog run freely on firm but soft areas, like grass or the wet sand on a beach.

Free running on a good surface is much safer, and puppies can fly around pretty freely on this, for much longer. Always be ready to lasso your pup and put him back on lead for a while to prevent him tiring himself out. A small puppy may appreciate a ride in your arms till she gets her second wind. And don't let her try to keep up with fast dogs!

I'll add here jumping - particularly in and out of cars. Heavier dogs need to be lifted in - and most particularly out - of cars. You may need a box or step to help them. Those shoulder joints - the growth plates at the top of the bones - can easily get damaged with repeated stress. This is why agility competitions are limited to dogs over 18 months of age.

Pulling into a collar and lead is not going to do your puppy any favours. A well-fitted harness should be used from the outset - not just to help with Loose Lead Walking but for physical safety.

Stairs? I teach my puppies to go up one step at a time, slowly. And they learn to come down the same way, going right to the bottom without jumping. If you have a heavy breed of dog you need to carry him up and down stairs for his first few months.

The growth plates close with sexual maturity, somewhere around 9-18 months of age. This is another reason for delaying any neutering till then. As this is a book for new puppies, I'm not discussing neutering except to say that it shouldn't be contemplated till the dog is sexually mature. For bitches that would mean a few months after the first season. Dogs would need to be 10 months to 3 years, depending largely on the size of the breed. The larger the dog, the longer it takes to mature. There are lots of reasons to delay neutering, which have little to do with reproduction.

Either way, you need to keep a lid on exercise for now, tempting though it may be to take your dog on a great family outing for several hours.

Is exercise what walks are for?

Free-running walks, and playing in the garden, are for exercise. Walking on a lead, on the road, is not!

So why do we walk dogs on the road on a lead? Good question! Mainly this is because of a total misunderstanding of the nature of proper exercise. But it does have a purpose - especially for a puppy!

Your roadwalks are for Socialisation, and once your puppy has a few months under her belt, they're for training. Lead-walking is when you can introduce your puppy to the world around you. Don't expect to get very far on these walks. You may know what it's like taking a toddler for a walk … you aren't looking to get anywhere fast! Your toddler has to inspect every leaf and snail on the way, and may decide to sit down and not budge at all.

Your puppy is the same! And when he sits down and won't budge this is nothing to do with being "stubborn" or "obstinate" or "opinionated" as is often suggested to me. He's either worn out, or simply unsure. That mark on the road may be a crocodile pit ahead, and the reflection off that plastic sack is very suspicious. So let him wait, keeping your lead slack, and let him move on when he's ready. Just wait. It won't be for long. You haven't got a train to catch!

Remember who this walk is for. And allow plenty of time to be flexible.

Play

Free play in a safe space is the perfect exercise. Running, a little jumping, chasing, digging, rolling - all good stuff.

Playing with toys - this is such an important part of bonding with you (and the kids). Just keep in mind your puppy's age when you play. Keep the toy low and only pull as much as he does - or just let him pull against you. Don't yank him about, swing him in the air, let him jump from unsuitable heights, or play to exhaustion. Keep the weather and temperature in mind too. Overheating is very dangerous for pups.

Playing with other dogs - see Chapter 3 for more about this. As far as exercise is concerned, ensure the play is equal, there are plenty of time-outs - maybe after three minutes or so have a break - the dogs are physically matched, and that breed or type differences in play are accommodated. Some love chasing and being chased, some like to body-slam and crash on top of each other, some like to leg-bite ... Play between two pups or maybe three is preferable. Large groups of puppies in a small room tends to be a recipe for disaster. You should always be able to call your puppy out of play.

These two puppies are free to interact or not as they wish

Indoors or outdoors?

Outdoors in a big space is always preferable. But of course it's not always possible. When playing indoors, ensure you clear a bit of space for the puppy so he can't crash into things, and consider the flooring. Smooth floors are great for keeping clean, but you'll need to put down a mat or two where your pup is likely to run or corner fast. Slipping could be bad news.

Retrieve, fetch, bring …

One way to get a lot of running done is by teaching a retrieve (see Resources) early on. This doesn't mean that you can endlessly launch balls for your dog as soon as you get outside. Teaching retrieve will ensure that you can interact *more* with your dog on walks, not less! It's a great skill that will enhance your life with your dog, so for now look to playing with toys with him as early as possible, to encourage him to use his mouth to explore and carry stuff.

Walking nicely on the lead

And while we're looking at teaching your puppy, be sure to use a kind program for teaching Loose Lead Walking from the outset. If you use my system you can get a lot of the preparatory work with your very young puppy done in the house, from 8 weeks old … without even using a lead!

Your puppy won't just automatically learn how to walk nicely on the lead. You have to show him what you want, and let him discover why he likes it. You don't want to be forever buying new gear and gadgets to force him to stop pulling. You want him to learn not to pull in the first place! So much easier. Check out the book *Let's Go!* in the Resources Section, and get started right away. Your shoulders and back will be so glad - over the next 15 years or so - that you did!

All Day Training

And as you'll see, there's no need to have dedicated training sessions or classes for these. And no need for squawking in frustration as your puppy runs off with the toy, lies down and chews it, or simply ignores it. And definitely no need for endlessly tramping round a field or hall in the hope that your dog will get it and not pull on the lead. Both these skills are taught as part of All Day Training. A little here, a little there. A treat for picking something up - then immediately a treat for dropping it to get the first treat! A treat for your puppy coming to your side in the kitchen, another for staying at your side for just one step. This is how you begin. It could hardly be simpler!

TROUBLESHOOTING

Q We don't have a garden

A This is unfortunate and will also make housetraining harder. But it's not impossible to manage. If you have space indoors, make sure it's suitably covered with carpet or large non-slip mats, with no sharp furniture edges to bean your puppy, and let rip indoors. You can take your puppy to suitable places to run free. Free play is essential for healthy development, in mind and body.

Q I want to walk my dog to the shops, where I can tie him up outside. This is ok, right?

A NO! I would never leave any dog - still less a puppy - tied up unattended. There are so many disasters that can befall this unfortunate dog, theft being only one of them. So only walk your dog to shops you can take him into. There are plenty of shops that will welcome dogs - butchers, greengrocers, banks, cafés, hardware shops, charity shops, post offices - so you can still have your walks. These will be great for socialising your puppy (don't let him be flooded with people saying "Aaaah!") as long as it's not too far for him to walk. If so, you can carry him part of the way, or use a stroller.

Q I have an older dog. I want them to be able to play all day together.

A For bonding with each dog you need to keep them separate a good part of the day, and play, walk, train, and interact with them individually. If you expect your older dog to train your younger dog you are abdicating your responsibilities - and you will be sadly disappointed. Their play may be good … or not. It depends on the comparative size of the dogs, the older dog's tolerance, their style of play. Supervise in the same way you would if you had two small children playing together.

Q My puppy still seems to have bags of energy, even after an active play session or walk.

A He's probably living on nervous energy now! After any exercise, your puppy needs to go down for a rest. It's not just to rest his body, but it's so he can process all that new information.

In this chapter we have learnt:

- The type of exercise you should aim for
- How to use up energy safely
- Walking nicely on the lead
- "I'm tired from all that running … where's my bed?"

5. Feeding

This is a minefield!

There's a lot of nonsense talked about dog feeding. Some of it is marketing hype. Some of it is passionate crusading. What we need is commonsense!

What it all boils down to is that you want the best food possible for your dog, that fits your budget, and that suits your lifestyle.

And there is guidance out there - unbiassed guidance. I'll give you some pointers here, and you'll find links in the Resources section to take you further.

Day 1

When you first bring your puppy home you should have a diet sheet provided by your breeder, along with all the info about what wormers etc he has had. And it is important to stick to this same feeding regime for at least the first week, while your puppy settles in with you. You don't want to add potential tummy upsets (which can be serious in a young puppy) to all the things he has to cope with when he arrives with you.

Many breeders get free packs of food from manufacturers to wean their puppies onto then pass on to new owners, telling them they shouldn't change. This is a clever marketing ploy by the manufacturers, who now have 8 new customers! There's nothing wrong with this, but you have to assess the quality of the food, not just its price, when you look at your puppy's diet.

Just as with babies, it's essential that your pup gets the right nutrients early on in his life, to ensure a strong skeleton and healthy body in the future. So it really is worth looking into this early on.

How do I change my puppy's food?

You'll need to visit some of the suggested Resources to decide on what food is right for you and your household. Even though you may live somewhere else, I would recommend the UK site suggested: it's not just a list of foods, but it explains what you should look for, and why - and, importantly, how to assess the food your puppy has arrived with. A lot of the dogfood manufacturers are global businesses, so the same foods will appear almost everywhere, albeit with slightly different names. Put on your deerstalker and puff on your pipe while you work it all out.

Change your puppy to your chosen new food gradually - over a week or so, adding a little more of the new food each day. Keep an eye on what's coming out the other end. It should always be firm and sausage-shaped, not sloppy like a cow-pat. If you've upgraded to a better food, there should be less cow-pats!

What to feed?

There's kibble (dry little biscuits in a big sack), wet food (in pouches or cans), home-cooked food (some available commercially), leftovers, and raw food, or a combination diet. No wonder you're confused!

- *Kibble*

This is undoubtedly the most convenient. What could be easier than having a big sack of dry food, which lasts for ages if protected from vermin and damp, and shovelling some into your dog's bowl each day?

There are hundreds of different varieties. Beware, many of the poorer ones are from those few global companies, operating under many different brand names. But there are also good ones. It's up to you to do that research and find out the best foods, then the best that will fit your budget.

Just because you can pick up a bag of dog food in the local store for less than the same-sized bag of woodshavings, doesn't mean you should get it! In most of your life you do not choose by price alone - even if you're watching the pennies - so don't inflict the cheapest food on your dog and expect him to do well on it.

And, when you've chosen a few suitable foods, I would rotate through the brands so that your dog isn't stuck with the same food, day in, day out, for ever. We're all different, and if I ate the exact same diet that you thrive on I may be short of some nutrient, or get too much of it. Dogs are the same, and no commercial dogfood can cater equally for all dogs. So mix and match and change things around from time to time.

Some vets promote expensive brands of kibble which they sell themselves. I have asked a number of vets who I have got to know when they came to me for training with their own puppy, "What do you learn in Vet School about canine nutrition?" The answer is usually a blank shake of the head - except for one vet who said, "We had a dogfood sales rep come to speak to us one morning." I rest my case. You have to do your own research.

Poor quality food can obviously result in loss of condition, stary dry coat, poor development, and so on. But it will also cause bulky loose stools. Change to a better food and you'll find picking up after your dog becomes so much easier and less frequent!

- *Wet food*

Some people like to feed something that looks more like food to them. And there are some products that are good quality, made from real food. But many are extruded stuff made to look like chunks of meat, drowned in a cereal-based gravy. By all means feed wet food if you and your dog prefer it, but all the caveats still apply. Buyer beware!

- *Home-cooked food*

This could be an excellent solution - though you do need to know what you're doing, and it could involve a lot of extra work for you.

UK readers can get a high-quality "home-cooked" food available commercially (see Resources).

- *Leftovers*

Well … this depends on what you leave. If your family eats a healthy diet with plenty of first-class protein and little junk, that may go some way towards feeding your pup. If you're a pizza-and-chips household though, forget it.

And if your food is good you're only going to have enough left over for a very small dog!

- *Raw food*

This is an increasingly popular choice - especially amongst dog professionals and performance dog-owners (think Agility, Flyball, Gundogs and the like). It doesn't mean you have to slaughter an ox every month and prepare it all yourself! There are plenty of manufacturers of raw dog food - some who operate on a fairly local basis, some large-scale - who serve you up convenient packs of prepared food to put straight into the freezer. You can also get plenty from your local butchers.

It's important to know what to feed, so check Resources for a reference for you. You don't want to feed all muscle meat as that will lead to imbalances and health issues. The raw diet should be 50% bone, as you'll see.

I have found puppies who come to class with runny tummies and poor, scrawny, condition, become like new after two weeks on a raw diet. As it's a natural food for the dog you can usually change straight over without that "honeymoon" period. But there's no harm in erring on the side of caution and changing over a week.

- *Combination*

Of course you can mix and match, and feed all of these things. But with a young puppy you don't want to make sudden or violent changes. As he grows up you can start giving him a bigger variety of quality food.

A popular idea is to offer a tray with a variety of different ingredients in little heaps. This could be cooked broccoli, raw chicken wing, cream cheese, offal, blueberries - all good stuff … And you could be very surprised at what he chooses to eat first!

It all boils down to you finding a feeding system that is convenient for your lifestyle and your pocket, and which gives your new dog the best you can offer for health and longevity.

Vegetarian or Vegan?

You may be a vegetarian, but your dog is not. They don't process carbohydrates well though they can utilise fats and protein. You only need to look at the jaws (scissor bite, no possibility of grinding vegetation and grains like we do with salivation and pre-digestion in the mouth), teeth (front teeth for ripping, canines for killing, molars for slicing, crunching, splitting and snapping), simple digestive system (it either goes down, or comes up again), to see that they are carnivores. I wouldn't feed a horse rump steak just because I liked it! My son fed dead mice to his snake: yuk … but who are we to judge a snake? You have to feed a species-specific diet.

You can introduce a raw chicken wing to a young puppy and get an instant visceral response: "This is REAL food!" By the way, your puppy's first bone may result in growling over it. This is not a resource guarding problem developing. Just leave her in peace in her crate to eat it, keeping an eye out. I never leave my dogs alone when I feed them anything, just in case something goes down the wrong way …

Read the label!

When you're checking out a possible food for your dog (check those sites in the Resources section!) you'll find the labels explained for you. You don't have to have a degree in canine nutrition to feed your dog properly!

Have a look at one of the lower-rated (but probably hugely popular) foods. A quick read of the label will usually say something like this:

"Composition: Cereals, Derivatives of Vegetable Origin, Meat and Animal Derivatives (including 4% Beef), Various Sugars, Vegetable Protein Extracts, Minerals, Seeds, Oils and Fats, Herbs, Preservatives"

Really? This is for feeding a carnivore? Who knows what all these ingredients actually are! And by the way, when it says "Beef" it doesn't specify which part of the animal it comes from … hooves? ears?

And when this list is for a chew product sold for promoting tooth health - it's a bit staggering. The first ingredient in this list is cereal (it often is, even in kibble), and cereal turns to sugar in the body. It also has added sugars. And we all know that sugar and teeth are a bad mix.

Compare with this label for a high-quality kibble:

"Composition: Chicken 19%, Chicken 18% (from Dried Chicken), Salmon 15%, Herring 12.5% (from Dried Herring, Sweet Potato 12%, Chicken Fat 4.5%, Duck 4% (from Dried Duck), Tapioca 3.5%, Whole Egg 2.5% (from Dried Egg), Chicken Liver 2.5%, White Fish 2%, Pea Fibre 2%, Lucerne,

Chickpea, Minerals & Vitamins, Carrot, Spinach, Apple, Rosehips, Camomile, Burdock Root, Seaweed, Cranberry, Aniseed & Fenugreek, Fructooligosaccharides (461 mg/kg), Glucosamine (341mg/kg), MSM (341mg/kg), Chondroitin (240mg/kg), Thyme, Marjoram, Oregano, Parsley, Sage"

All the ingredients are named and specified. The percentages are totally geared towards a broad diet for a carnivorous animal. There is no comparison with the poorer-quality food above. And just so you know, the better the product does not necessarily mean the higher the price. Keep in mind though that the better the product, the less you need to feed, as it's all good nutrition and not indigestible fillers that will come straight out again as poo.

Many manufacturers have different feeds for different age-groups or sizes of dog. I've even seen foods for specific breeds!

You don't feed different food to your baby or children - you may mash it or cut it up, but you feed them FOOD! The same food you eat. So I think this is just a marketing ploy. If you're feeding a good quality diet and monitoring the results, you're good.

It's true that some breeds require a diet particularly low or high in something (the breeder will explain this to you), but this doesn't need to restrict your choices.

How much should I feed?

If you go for a bag of kibble, there will be feeding suggestions on the pack. Take these as a *rough* guide. We're all different - you and I could end up completely different sizes on the same intake!

You need to develop a "stockman's eye". Run your eyes and your hands over your dog regularly. Can you see and feel the ribs? Seeing them will be difficult in a fluffy pup but you should be able to feel them clearly. You don't want to cut yourself on them, but you should definitely be able to locate individual ribs. Can you feel the pin bones at the top of the pelvis above the hind legs? They should slightly protrude. And are there hard rolls of fat on the back of the neck under the collar? There should be loose skin there, but it should be empty!

If all those checks are right, then you're feeding the right amount. Remember to remove an equivalent amount of food from the daily allowance for treats given in training. And as you're feeding real food for treats, and not the junk with labels like the first one above, that's fine.

Treats

Use the exact same criteria for treats as you do for your dog's main foods. Commercial treats are often huge, sugary confections which are no use at all. Make your own! Chop some cheese, or some cocktail sausages or hot dogs, into tiny cubes, like half-a-pea-size. They'll keep for quite some time in the fridge. You can bake treats for your puppy if you like - plenty of resources on the web for simple, healthy, recipes. But make sure you're only feeding real food!

If you're concerned that your puppy is getting too much, then do NOT cut down the rewards! Take a little of his daily ration out of his bowl instead.

You'll see in this book and my other, step-by-step, books, that you'll get through a lot of treats during the day. I only give my dogs a treat when they've done something I like - whether asked for or not. I aim to dish out a lot of treats each day!

How should I feed my puppy?

Now here's a big question - a huge opportunity to bond with your new pup, and it's often completely overlooked!

I feed most of my puppy's food by hand. Yep, by hand. If his food is wet, use your fingers or a teaspoon; if it's raw, use poultry shears to cut it into very small pieces you can dish out one by one. Don't be squeamish - you're feeding a species-appropriate diet! Vegan and vegetarian friends of mine do just this.

So most of his meals will be hand-fed in return for a little interaction or perhaps one of my training games (in the books - see Resources). Then some will be fed in a foodtoy of some kind. (Use real food in these! Don't be seduced by some commercial gunk with a huge shelf-life and no nutrition!). Sometimes I scatter-feed - just sprinkle his food on the floor or, even better, on the lawn (not on a stony drive), and let him hunt and hoover it up. Maybe once a day he gets his meal in a bowl or container of some kind.

My dogs enjoying a scattered breakfast on holiday, while I eat mine from a bowl.

While your puppy needs regular meals, you can space them out to suit your own timetable. Don't feed immediately before or after exercise, or when a thirsty dog has just drunk a bucket of water. This is a rough guide to the number of meals your puppy needs.

8 to 12 weeks:	4 meals a day
12-16 weeks:	3 meals a day
6 months:	2 meals a day
9-12 months:	you can cut down to 1 if you both like

Food toys

Food toys are the best thing ever. If you haven't already got some for your puppy, go and buy them now! They help to slow down feeding in a ravenous gobbler, they entertain your pup when you need him to be quiet for a while, the calm licking and sucking will send him off to sleep in his crate. Until you're sure your puppy has sussed out how to get the food out without trying to eat the container, stay near him.

You can improvise food toys too. No small box is thrown away here, without having some treats tossed in and given to one of the dogs. They love ripping it apart to find their prize! Plastic bottles with some treats in and a bit of kitchen paper loosely pushed in can take a while for them to solve (not for heavy-duty chewers and demolition agents). A well-chewed raw marrow bone can have some cheese or liver pate squashed into it for them to get out. Be imaginative!

So what do I feed my own dogs?

My own dogs are largely fed a raw diet. This consists of chicken carcases, bones that they can chew up - not marrowbones or load-bearing leg bones, which are often too hard - turkey wings, offal of all sorts (liver, kidney, heart, tripe, lung), pigs' trotters, eggs smashed into the bowl. There are packs of commercially-prepared raw food (lamb, fish, beef) which will give them more variety.

They get some leftovers of good food, cooked vegetables included, and some liquidised fruit (dogs can't break down cellulose so it has to be broken down for them). They enjoy coming blackberrying with me, and pick their own!

On the rare occasions I've forgotten to defrost their food they may get a high-quality kibble, often with egg or sardines mixed in. And I have high-quality canned food, kibble, and packs of conveniently-packaged commercial raw or home-cooked food for travelling in the van.

I like to give them a variety of food. I'd get bored silly if given the same food only, day in, day out. So if, for any reason, I had to feed only kibble, I'd rotate through a few of the best-quality feeds to ensure a variety of nutrients and tastes.

The result of this diet? My dogs all live to a vigorous old age (15-17 years usually). They die with all their teeth which are largely white, and they never get any of those degenerative diseases so common in dogs today. We only visit the vet if there's an injury needing treatment. Otherwise we never see him …

I put this down to diet, and suitable exercise.

This meaty bone will keep Coco engaged for hours

TROUBLESHOOTING

Q My puppy's stools are very loose and sloppy

A First stop: Vet. You need to check for bacterial or parasitic infection. When you're sure your pup is clean, start studying the available foods. Change him slowly over a week. Once you've got the right food, your puppy's stools should be firm, sausage-shaped, and much less frequent!

Q I tried a different food but my puppy won't eat it

A Did you change gradually over a week, adding a little more of the new food each day? Are you sure he ate none of it? Or did he just eat a lot less than on a previous food? In that case, he's getting enough of what he needs from a smaller amount. If he won't touch it at all, then perhaps it's not for him. If it's kibble, the nuts may be too big for his mouth or are too hard: soften with water for a while before feeding. But a healthy puppy won't starve to death!

As long as you're sure he doesn't have any health issues (Vet check!) and you know it's a superior food, you can try him a little longer on it. You could always spice it up to begin with by adding some shredded chicken, tinned sardines, egg - whatever he likes, just to get him started.

Q Did you say you feed chicken bones? I was always told you shouldn't do this!

A Good, and frequent, question! RAW bones of any kind can be fed and chewed and swallowed. It's *cooked* bones, which become brittle and more likely to splinter, that you must avoid. I've been feeding raw to my many dogs over 35 years or so - that's over a hundred years worth of dog-feeding! - and have *never* had a bone-related problem. There was once, in all those years, when a puppy wolfed down a large lump of boned chicken and I had to fish it out of her throat for her (as I said, I don't leave the dogs alone to feed). I learnt that meat attached to a bone is safer! They quickly learn to chomp and crunch before they swallow. You may need to hold your puppy's first chicken wing so he realises he has to bite with the side of his jaw and not just try to wolf it all down in one go.

Q The man in the pet shop said I should get his own-brand food - but the site you recommend doesn't rate it highly.

A The man in the pet shop may be lovely and helpful, but the bottom line is … it's his bottom line! He needs to stay in business so he's likely to recommend the best deal for him. The advice in the site I recommend (Resources) is independent and unbiassed, and is not affected by your choice. You have to live with your dog for the next 12-15 years. How much better for everyone if your dog is healthy and happy and never has to visit the vet? Think of how much money you save by not having to get veterinary treatment! You can buy many bags of top-quality food for each visit saved.

In this chapter we have learnt:

- What you can feed your dog
- Different types of foods
- Different ways to feed
- "Food toys keep me busy for ages."

6. Jumping up!

So many people want to stop their dog jumping up - on them, on worktops, on visitors. Now you're getting well into this book, you'll have a sneaky feeling what the answer to this one is!

> *Instead of trying to stop your dog doing something, rather teach him what you'd like him to do instead.*

If he has something he can do and knows it will please you, he won't need to do all the things you find annoying when he would like your attention. Or when he wants to greet you.

Why does my puppy want to jump up in the first place?

It's natural for a puppy to try to reach your face with a "kiss" - that's how they greet their dam in the nest. When she returns after a hunt, the puppies will all reach up and lick her face and teeth, to prompt her to regurgitate her kill.

Now we don't feel the need to throw up our last meal for our puppy, so we want to teach a new, mutually satisfying, greeting protocol for you and your hapless visitors.

What most people do

- Make sure dog is super-excited and racing around loose, barking
- Shout "Get off! Stop! NO!", wave arms, dance, add to the excitement
- Give dog lots of attention for jumping on people and no attention whatever when his feet are on the floor
- Make sure dog knows that wherever he goes and whatever he does, it's WRONG

Hmm. You already know that's not going to work! So what do you do instead?

What YOU're going to do

One way to prevent your puppy jumping up is to get down to his level first! This gives you the opportunity to slip a finger in his collar so he can't jump while you cuddle and canoodle.

Another regular winner is to focus him on keeping his feet on the floor. If you haven't yet got a solidly-trained Sit, you can just stand and wait for him to work out that jumping is not doing the trick and he'll either stand or sit without you having to say a word!

> *Be sure you don't reward his jumping with cries of "Off! Get down! Ouch!" which he will take to mean "I love this! Keep jumping!"*

For a slightly older puppy who has already been well-rewarded for his jumping, a good way to intercept him is to slide your thumb down his neck and into his collar or harness, keeping your arm straight, and gently lowering both of you to the ground to greet.

A surefire way to focus attention downwards is simply to place a treat on the floor between his feet - this will get him to look floorwards. Now another treat, now another - keep 'em coming. He can't be staring at the floor at the same time as jumping up, so the problem is eliminated.

By getting your puppy to choose to do a different action, this will work to keep your pup's feet on the floor and off you - without having to admonish or scold him for his enthusiasm.

> *Remember that if you don't want something to happen, you don't let it happen - be proactive! Then you can reward your pup for doing what you want.*

Much more fun to direct your puppy to something you *do* like, rather than continually nagging him and focussing on what you *don't* like.

Remember to practice this at all times of the day. Don't wait till you have visitors to fuel the excitement! To start with it'll be enough to cope with your puppy's excitement at being with you.

> *And always remember that what you **reward** is what you get! And a reward can be food, attention, noise, interaction …*

First law of feet on the floor

No-one - family, visitors, or strangers on the street - may interact with the puppy at all unless all his four feet are on the floor.

This gets easier as time goes by, and you'll have a shorter and shorter time to wait before you can address your pup. Start on Day 1, at eight weeks old! No attention is given till feet are all on the floor. Appear to be completely uninterested in this jumping, wiggling, thing - while you watch out of the corner of your eye. The split second the front feet arrive on the floor you reward with attention - down at his level. Don't ask for a sit or anything else.

He'll learn very fast! You don't have to say NOOO or OFFFF or GEDDOWN or anything at all. Just stay still and wait for him to pause for a second. Then respond immediately! It's essential to catch the moment the feet hit the floor so that he knows *exactly* what he did that got your attention.

1. Puppy wants to greet you.
2. Stand still and wait, looking away.
3. The split second his front feet hit the floor, mark the exact moment "YES!" and do one of the actions suggested above.

All this requires is patience on your part while your puppy does the learning.

Jumping up at visitors

Now you can't expect your visitors to do this training for you! They need to be protected from scrabbling paws and playfully snapping jaws. Here's a step-by-step sequence to making this work - every time.

1. To contain the flying excitement, clip a lead onto your puppy's collar and put your foot on the lead so that he's still free to sit, stand or lie down, but can't jump up. (We're not slamming him to the floor - he has to have a choice!)

2. Greet your guest and ask them to ignore the puppy.

3. If he's keeping (more or less) still, he gets the opportunity to say hello to your guest - as long as his feet stay on the floor. Now he's learning how to greet visitors politely. So when your dog is sitting or standing patiently, ask your guest to hold their palm out for the dog to sniff. You can either slide your lead-anchoring foot forward so he can reach the hand but still can't jump, or just let him move forward without that restraint.

4. Reward your dog with a treat and gushing praise as you draw him gently back to your side.

Practice makes Perfect - so try this out with a friend who is prepared to wait outside the door while you take your time and calmly lead up your dog without having to worry about someone waiting for you. If you flap and start yelling "Hang on!" this excitement will without doubt transfer to your puppy!

You could practice each stage with your friend, so that if your dog tries to leap up when the door opens to reveal the visitor, you can simply close the door gently in front of him, and open it again when he's calmed down a bit and is giving you a sit and/or eye contact.

> *Your dog will soon understand that it's his good choices that enable you to open the door and admit the visitor! This is empowering for a young puppy - learning about cause and effect in the best way possible. Such empowerment will have him making those good decisions over and over again.*

Your regular visitors will be astonished and amazed, and glad that they're now able to wear ordinary clothes to visit you instead of disposable overalls.

You'll be so glad when you can welcome a visitor to your home without them getting mobbed! You'll be proud of what you've achieved, proud of your dog, and relieved that you're no longer the big bad shouting joy-killer.

Cleverclogs stuff: later on you can teach him to go to his bed near the door when the doorbell rings, and stay till invited off (you'll find out how in my free book *Calm Down! Step-by-step to a Calm, Relaxed, and Brilliant Family Dog* - see Resources section). This will impress your visitors no end, and keep everything nice and calm and quiet.

Impulse Control

All this is helping to build your puppy's impulse control. Impulse control is what we all have to learn to fit in with society and not drive everyone mad. Your puppy will learn this too, and the sooner he does, the better.

> *And the joy of Choice Training is that you have to do very little in order for your puppy to learn this self-control.*

Leave It! (see Resources) gives you a complete program to teach your puppy to leave shoes, sleeves, food, dropped items, the toddler's biscuit, rubbish, yukky stuff, etc. Until you embark on that program, you can ensure that your puppy always has to give you something before getting something himself:

- He wants attention? Feet on the floor.
- He wants food? Wait for the bowl without jumping
- He wants out to the garden? Wait till door is opened, then release him

> *You do something for me, you get what you want.*

TROUBLESHOOTING

Q My puppy is very small so jumping up is the only way he can reach me.

A Getting down to his level - even picking him up if he likes it - will work for you. Be sure you don't wait for him to jump up first then reward him with attention! This is creating what we trainer-folk call a "behaviour chain" - first I do this, then this, then that happens. Think of cleaning your teeth in the morning - first you pick up the brush, then you anoint it with toothpaste, then you brush. You can't do the brushing without the first step! And you'd probably find it hard, through force of habit, to miss out the toothpaste. So eliminate the jumping step and cut straight to the greeting.

Q My puppy is huge and heavy - he's going to be enormous when full grown!

A So you certainly want to sort this now. Don't wait till he's not quite as cute and rather more weighty before working on this. That wouldn't be very fair on him, would it? It'll be easy for you to reach him if he's that big, so he never learns he needs to jump up. Apart from anything else, jumping up puts too much strain on a large breed's skeleton. Some savvy breeders of large dogs put up a partial barrier *above* puppy height at the front of the pen, so in order to see you the puppy has to keep his feet on the floor! Job done.

Q I don't want to squash his enthusiasm

A Absolutely not! I love an enthusiastic greeting from my own dogs. You just have to show them what works and what doesn't. You don't need to complain, nag, or tell off your puppy. Just wait for the action you want and reward that with your attention.

Q But I like my dogs putting their paws up on me!

A So do I! And I can invite all mine to do that - when I want it. That'll be when I know their feet are dry and not muddy; when my hands aren't full of something delicate, hot, or dangerous; when I'm in the mood. That's why I put jumping up on cue - so I can get it when I want it. I've also made it into a "trick" - when I ask for a hug, they'll sit and put their front paws on my thigh. It's very cute, especially when all four do it at once!

In this chapter we have learnt:

- Why puppies jump up
- What you're not going to do, and what you ARE going to do to change this
- How to handle visitors
- "I can still love people without lepping about!"

7. Housetraining

A word about crates

As a crate is one of the most useful pieces of kit you can get for your new puppy, let's get something out of the way first:

- "It's cruel to put a puppy in a crate"
- "We do have a crate, but we never shut the door"
- "I don't want him to see his crate as a punishment"
- "We're saving money by getting a crate that will fit him when he's full-grown"

These are common responses I hear when I ask owners if they have a crate for their puppy.

My thoughts:

- Do you think it's cruel to put a baby in a cot or playpen?
- Would you leave your toddler loose in the house at night without supervision?
- I bet your child's bed is full of cuddly toys, books, comforters, and he's happy there
- Do your children look like extras from St.Trinian's, with their jumpers down to their knees so you can save money?

The only way a crate would be cruel would be if your puppy were left locked in it all day. The same would hold true for leaving a child in a cot or playpen all day! The crate is an excellent help for keeping a puppy safe in his new home, and is your best friend when it comes to housetraining - and to getting a good night's sleep.

So now we've got those misunderstandings cleared up, you're ready to set off on your Errorless Housetraining - with the crate doing a lot of the work for you!

The two keys to success

For total success with your puppy's housetraining, much faster than you might expect, you're going to take advantage of two important facts about puppies:

1. Puppies need to sleep a minimum of 17 hours a day

Seventeen hours is what adult dogs need. So a puppy will obviously need more. It's a lot more sleep than many new owners allow their puppy, and they're amazed to find that a lot of minor irritations and things they considered problem behaviours can be resolved by simply ensuring sufficient downtime. *All that sleep needs to take place in your pup's crate.* So when it's time for a rest (after maybe one hour of activity) you take your puppy to bed, shut the crate door, and leave him to settle. Half-cover the crate with a blanket so it's a cosy den. You can feed all your dog's meals in his crate so he's always happy to go there, and when you leave him, give him a food-toy or something he can safely chew.

2. A well-reared puppy will not soil his bed

This is why you want to get a crate that is the right size for him now. If you must get a giant crate for your little puppy, block off the greater part of it with the custom divider or cardboard boxes - it doesn't matter if your puppy shreds the boxes. We want his sleeping area just big enough for him to lie down, stand up, and turn round. Just as our beds aren't enormous - they just fit us for sleeping. Always leave safe chew toys so he has something to amuse him as he nods off. Licking a food-toy is soothing. Classical music - especially Mozart - playing on the radio is calming to many dogs and can block out other household sounds.

Housetraining is a management issue!

Housetraining is not your puppy's job, it's yours! Your puppy is going to need to wee and poo. Frequently. Your job is simply to make sure it all happens where you want it to - i.e. outside. You need to be taking him out, on a lead, much more often than you think! Every half hour is a good rule of thumb, and even more often if your little puppy is active and playing.

You need to keep him on lead until he's done his business, then you can let him off to explore the garden and play with you. Why? If you take him out without a lead, he's more likely to bounce about chasing butterflies and sniffing leaves, so that when you get bored and bring him back in, he still has a full bladder or bowels. Keeping him on lead focusses his attention on what he needs to do.

Your puppy will gradually earn his freedom in the house as he shows that he can perform immediately when you take him outside. For now he should always be in your sight, in the same room as you, OR safely confined.

People are sometimes baffled that their puppy is still not housetrained after many months - they tell me they leave the door open for him all the time. This is why he's not done yet! He will continue to pee wherever he happens to be. Sometimes that's outside and you're happy, and sometimes it's inside, and you're not. How baffling for him! You need to show him that he goes outside for this purpose, and he won't learn if he can wander in and out, chasing those butterflies, whenever he wants. He needs to understand the sequence of feeling the need, going outside and then relieving himself.

Sniffing the ground can be a precursor to weeing, as circling is to pooing

No paper please - apartment dwellers

Another wrong turning people may take - especially if they've been taking their advice from uninformed friends or the local pet shop - is to use paper pads for their puppy to eliminate on. How is this puppy going to learn that this should take place outside?

I have known people who live in high-rise flats - where it would be impossible to race down the stairs with a puppy every few minutes! - successfully use an indoor toiletting arrangement. But this needs to be a particular, clearly-bordered area (like a giant tea-tray) in a specific place - perhaps the bathroom, or on a balcony. You can use paper or artificial grass you can wash down. This puppy will also need to be taught to use the great outdoors too when on walks. Taking some of the used paper and spreading it on the grass at a suitable location may help to trigger a wee outside. Allowing the dog to do much sniffing so he can "cover" another dog's pee may also work well.

I expect my pups to be clean and dry by night at 7-9 weeks, and by day at 8-12 weeks. A puppy who is still not housetrained at 17 weeks is one who has developed habits which you will now have to change. How much easier to start off doing it right and not letting these poor habits develop!

Poo problems

If your puppy's poos are loose and frequent, head over to Chapter 5 Feeding and check out how to change this (with a vet check first).

If she needs to poo in the night, or worse - does it in her crate! - you may need to adjust the timing of her meals. Feed some raw carrot with her meal, record the time, and notice when the orange chips emerge in her poo. Now you have an idea of the gut transit time. So you may need to bring your pup's last meal forward, or make it later, to allow for 8 hours of sleep.

Also be sure you're feeding the right number of meals for your pup's age (Chapter 5 again). Feeding too few meals can result in this problem.

"Good morning Beverley, Just had to let you know that I followed your guidance re settling Gertie at night and we had a peaceful sleep with no crying and no mess in her bed, a very big thank you." *Miniature Dachshund pup 11 weeks*

Fast-track your puppy to being clean and dry!
HOUSETRAINING CHEATSHEET

Housetraining is a management issue. Your puppy is going to eliminate, so it's up to you to make sure it all goes in the right place!

1. *Take your puppy out*

- As soon as she wakes
- Every time she's eaten
- Every time she's been drinking
- Every time she's been playing for more than five minutes
- .. and *every half hour while she's awake*

2. Take the puppy outside *on a lead* to your chosen area. Stand and be boring until puppy wees (usually less than a minute) and poos (sometimes three minutes). Allow her to sniff and circle. You may stroke the grass to encourage her to sniff. When she's done you can reward her with a treat, unclip the lead, have a game, and let her explore the great outdoors.

3. If nothing happens, take her back into the house and *pop her in her crate* with something to play with. Try again in ten minutes. If you let a pup free in the house when you know she needs to eliminate, you are guaranteeing failure!

4. Once she's doing this predictably as soon as you go outside, you can *start adding your chosen vocal cue* (I use "Hurry up"). Say it quietly just as your pup is performing - don't interrupt her! You'll know when your pup has "got this" when she starts to lick her lips as she pees, in anticipation of her treat.

5. *Don't use any paper or pads* in the house as it's confusing to the puppy - sometimes she may wee inside and other times not.

6. *Keep your pup in the same room as you*, and confine her when you're not able to supervise - either in a crate or penned area of a room with cleanable floor, like the kitchen. A well-reared puppy will not soil her own bedding, so fill up the crate with plenty of this. Unless the weather is scorching hot, no need to leave water in the crate.

7. *Be careful to show no emotion or annoyance* if you have a puddle to clear up. Your puppy will pick up on this and may decide that wee or poo and you in the same area are bad news and start going behind the sofa. I find the best cleaning product is biowash for the washing machine. Make up a solution in a spray bottle.

8 *Focus on this* for a couple of weeks. Act delighted when your pup performs outside! A half-hearted approach to housetraining means that it will drag on for weeks.

9. If you have a woolly, fluffy puppy, ensure her *anal area* is trimmed neatly and kept free from hair.

10. If you're starting with *an older dog*, perhaps a rescue, follow the *exact same steps*, except that you can take him out every hour, instead of half an hour.

TROUBLESHOOTING

Q My puppy won't relieve herself when we're out - only at home in the garden.

A Somehow you've built in the idea that the garden is the only place for her to eliminate. It's best to avoid this problem entirely when the puppy is very young and needs to wee frequently. If you already have this issue, don't despair! You can fix it by taking your puppy out on a lead as soon as she's eaten or at any other time you know she'll need a wee or poo. Wander around on a surface similar to your own garden (grass? paving?) and give her plentiful sniffing opportunities. You could even mop up a little of her wee at home with kitchen paper and bag it, then put it on the ground for her to sniff. Walking with a friend whose dog will happily use the outdoor facilities will often help.

Q I can wait 5 minutes outside in the freezing cold then she pees as soon as we get back in!

A Choose your moments to take her out carefully - and take a book, a coat, and a cup of tea with you! If she does nothing, then she goes back in her crate for ten minutes before you try again. You *are* keeping her on lead?

Q My puppy is so good at going in the garden - but when a visitor comes she pees on the floor

A This is not so much a pee as a loss of bladder control with the excitement of the visitor, or is to show submission. A puppy will often pee before an older dog, or even roll on her back to expose her genitals to be sniffed. This is from a sensible fear of the adult dog who will recognise the scent, know that she's only a puppy and is no threat. She'll grow out of this as she gains confidence.

Meanwhile, put her on lead and meet visitors outside then come in together after the initial excitement. You may need to help build her confidence round strangers (see Chapter 3 Socialisation).

Q My puppy *ate* some poo! It's disgusting!

A No, not disgusting. Just normal. She found something that smelled of food so she sampled it. If it was her own poo this is a sign that you need to improve her diet so that her food is properly digested (Chapter 5 Feeding). You also need to be with her and bag the product immediately and remove it, till her habit is broken and you've built a new, hygiene-conscious, habit! If it's other dogs' poo, there's a danger of parasitic infection, so be vigilant on walks and ensure it doesn't happen.

Q My puppy doesn't cock his leg - is there something wrong with him?

A Male dogs don't start lifting a leg till they're several months old. And an adult male may still squat to relieve himself. The leg-lifting is for marking - gateposts, trees, lampposts … Don't let your male mark everything you pass, and especially not doorways!

Q Why do I need to add a vocal cue for a natural function?

A It can be very useful when you're in a strange area to tell your dog that this is an ok time and place to eliminate - specially useful if you're travelling. You should also get an immediate result, so that is very useful. What words? Anything you feel happy saying in public for the next however-many years! I use the fairly innocuous "Hurry up". No need to have different words for pee and poo. As you are adding the label of what the puppy is doing *while* she's doing it, just the one word will cover it.

In this chapter we have learnt:

- It's up to us to manage the whole housetraining program
- Management of sleeping arrangements will help enormously
- How not to store up problems for the future
- "Aaaaah, that's better!"

8. Stealing and running off

Why does my puppy take things and run off?

Why do any of us do anything? Because we enjoy the activity or the result. Your puppy is the same.

Picture this: your puppy appears before you with your best shoe in her mouth and a glint in her eye. You reach forward with a shout to grab the shoe. Puppy realises she chose the right item to get your attention, spins on the spot and scampers away, turning and staring at you with that gleam again. You advance and try another grab. Pup hurtles off, leaps over the sofa, runs behind the armchair, peeps out to make sure you're still chasing, runs between your legs and races up the stairs. You are now annoyed and shouting louder. The whole episode ends in tears with you trapping the puppy and wrenching the shoe from her mouth, checking it over for damage.

Some questions:

- How come your puppy was able to access your best shoe?
- Where were you when she found it?
- Your puppy was awake: why weren't you paying attention?
- Did you know you were rewarding the puppy with massive attention for taking the shoe?
- Did you realise how you were teaching your puppy that picking something up and running off is a surefire way of getting that instant attention - and a great game!

Want to know how to change this?

1. Tidy up. Only leave things accessible that you don't much care about.

2. Always have the puppy in the same space as you, or in her crate.

3. Ensure there are plenty of toys and disposable objects (cartons, toilet roll tubes, etc) lying around in her crate, her toy basket, or on the floor while she's awake. Encourage her to pick these up and play with them.

4. Sit down with her and practice swapping anything she has in her mouth for a treat or another toy. *Always give the item back to her.*

5a. *If you have a history of stealing and chasing:* When she picks up a permitted item and looks at you, wondering if there's a game to be had, toss a treat down for her and don't accept the gauntlet.

5b. *If you haven't already got a stealing issue:* When she picks up a permitted item and looks at you, thank her, swap it for a treat, admire the item, *and give it back to her.*

6. By all means enjoy playing a chase game with her if you like - as long as it's with one of her toys. No need to take it off her - just run about and laugh. This game is known as "Keepaway" and is great fun. Ensure she's not afraid and the game always ends with treats or cuddles with you.

7. Always remember that your puppy is not trying to annoy you - *Dogs do what works!* Make sure that what you want works for your puppy too.

This is ordinary chase-play. If your puppy goes stiff over his stolen item, shows the whites of his eyes, wrinkles his lips, gives a low growl, you just may have a resource guarding issue. The best thing for you to do is to get professional help from a force-free trainer who can observe and show you how to change this easily and kindly.

I can't catch my puppy!

Sounds as if you've already taught this chase game well!

You should never have to "catch" your puppy. Your puppy should always be happy to come to you. How are you ever going to get a reliable recall when she's older if she's trying to avoid you now?

If there's a possible danger to the puppy - you're opening the street door to a visitor, for instance - you need to be proactive and do one of three things:

1. Pop her in her crate while you answer the door
2. Pick her up and hold her while you answer the door
3. Have her on a house line (an 8-foot light line) while you open the door

The Precious Name Game

Remember this valuable game from the Introduction? Go back and revise it. You want to play this with your puppy every single time you interact with her! Once she knows her name means treats, pleasure, affection, attention, you have the makings of a great solid recall later on.

Mayhem and destruction?

As you will have seen by now, this is not a by-product of having a puppy. Once you've put some safeguards and house rules in place, it becomes second nature to mind and protect your puppy.

And as you saw from Chapter 1 and Chapter 2, sleep is the great redeemer. If your puppy is going wild, biting, ripping, destroying things - it means she's *tired*. She needs an hour or two in her crate so she can rejoin you refreshed, calm and rational again. An overtired toddler is not amenable to reason - bed is the only answer. Your puppy is the exact same.

TROUBLESHOOTING

Q I don't want toys and stuff all over the floor.

A Don't be houseproud! Shredded cardboard is easy to clear up. You can shepherd all the toys into his basket or crate when he goes down for a sleep. (In a while you'll be teaching him to tidy up his toys himself!) Your dog lives with you now. Let him have what he needs to explore and learn safely.

Q How can I stop my puppy taking the children's toys?

A Good question! He can tell the difference between his toys and theirs very easily. Remember dogs work primarily through their noses (a third of the canine brain is devoted to scent). If he makes a mistake, just swap the child's toy for one of his own, and/or a treat. No big deal. Swap it, don't snatch it! Be sure there aren't tiny pieces of plastic unsafe for children under the age of three. These could wreak havoc with your puppy's insides. If he likes to rip and pull out the stuffing, discard the stuffing and give him the remaining glove toy.

Q My puppy doesn't steal things, but he wants to gnaw anything solid, like the table legs.

A Some puppies have a greater need or desire to chew than others. So provide whatever it is your puppy finds satisfying. If he wants something big and solid which gives a lot of resistance, a large bone would do the trick.

Q How will he learn a recall when free running on a walk if I play Keepaway with him at home?

A He'll learn a recall through the recall training games you'll play with him (Resources), and the fact that you are the best thing ever! For now don't worry unnecessarily. Just continue to build the unbreakable bond with your puppy by never telling him off or threatening him.

Q My puppy has a super recall - and she's only 9 weeks old!

A That's great to hear - but keep in mind that she's still a clingy baby. Once she builds her confidence (that's a *good* thing!) she'll explore more and you will need to *teach* a recall if you want it to continue this good. Think toddlers vs teenagers … you need to get the learning in early, it's much harder once they hit adolescence and say "Whywhywhy?"

In this chapter we learnt:

- Why your puppy is stealing things
- How you have taught him this game!
- How to teach a better game
- "I love playing this new game!"

9. Choosing a puppy, if you haven't yet done that!

You're reading this book - not because you have a puppy who is already driving you mad - but because you haven't yet got your puppy and you want to be fully prepared for this new relationship to blossom.

I love people like you! People who take seriously the choosing of a dog to share their lives with, and need to learn in advance how it's going to go. No spur-of-the-moment, grab-the-first-puppy-you-see for you.

So here's a guide to what you need to know to make the right decisions and not be taken for a ride by some unscrupulous puppy farmer who couldn't care less about the future of their pups - they're just commodities to be sold.

Narrowing down the choice

So the whole family has decided that you are going to get a puppy. Excitement is running high, and everyone has their own idea about this new family member.

Your older boy sees this new dog as a companion in his muddy adventures. Your younger girl views it as something to love and cuddle, brush and comb. You have fantasies about a dog curled up at your feet when your work is done and you at last hit the armchair. And perhaps your partner thinks of something butch and manly to show off at the pub from time to time, or to accompany him on long walks and fishing trips.

How on earth can you combine all this into one dog?

The truth is that while different breeds have different mindsets and hard-wired behaviours, the individual dog will have his own ideas. There is more variation between individual dogs than between breeds!

Just like when you have children you get what you're given, so with puppies. It doesn't matter how carefully you choose your puppy, he's still going to have a mind of his own. You could get a dog of an apparently outdoorsy breed who loves his bed more than anything. Or a lapdog who is feisty and needs constant stimulation. Look at different children in the same family! There's huge variation.

So you're going to need to do a bit of educating your family so that everyone is not disappointed with the new arrival. Find out what it is they are expecting, and guide them to more realistic expectations. Long walks can't happen till the pup is almost mature, for example. They'll all love the puppy just the same once it's arrived.

But choosing the right breed or type in the first place is a huge help!

The right dog for your family

You'll need to consider these points:

- Size
  Critical

The larger the dog the more expensive he'll be to feed, house, and take to the vet. Small dogs can be more inclined to jump up and scrabble (small child hazard) and can yap. Very large dogs need very large beds, very large cars, very large floorspace. (Deerhounds traditionally live in castles …)

- Coat-type
  Importance depends on your time and housekeeping standards

Double-coated dogs can shed year-round in our heated homes. Fluffy dogs will need a full groom every six weeks or so. (You can easily learn to do this yourself - the groomer's bills will add up alarmingly.) Long coats get muddy and tangled. Very fine-coated dogs get cold and need a jumper in the winter.

- Gender
  Not terribly important

When you've decided on your breed or type, you'll find that either dogs or bitches of that breed match your family better. They have very different characteristics, and of course size can vary a lot between the sexes. In some breeds, for example, the males tend to be soft and malleable, while the females can be prickly and moody - and sometimes the dog will be significantly larger and heavier than the delicate, feminine bitch. If you have an open mind you will have more choice in the litter. Don't factor in the possible cost of neutering - this is a distraction.

- Original purpose of the breed
  Critical

Hunting dogs (e.g. Labradors, Beagles, Spaniels) will go all day long in any weather. Lapdogs (like Shih Tsus, Chihuahuas) will expect a lap and as little weather as possible. Sighthounds (e.g. Whippets) want to sprint for ten minutes then sleep for 23 and a half hours. Herding dogs (Border Collies, German Shepherds, for example) are super-brainy and need constant stimulation. Jack Russell Terriers think they are German Shepherds. If your family is an outdoorsy one all year round, then you can get a dog used to striding over moors and mountain. If going to the shops is a big adventure for you, then something happy to mooch about at home is required. Be very honest about this.

- Age
  Absolutely critical

Your pup should be 7-8 weeks when he comes home with you. I would not take a puppy a day older. I'd walk away empty-handed - that's how important I consider this. And you should not take a puppy younger than 7 weeks, for any reason.

Visit your puppy at least once before you finally decide. 5-6 weeks is a good age to visit and see the pups' characters.

How to know the actual age of the puppies you're viewing? Either take a knowledgeable friend, or do a bit of preliminary study - Youtube will give you lots of videos to help you see what puppies are like at what age.

Your puppy's primary socialisation window slams shut at 14-16 weeks. You can never get this time back again. Greeders (you'll find out about them in a minute) will try and fob you off with a much older puppy who's been left behind. Do not listen to any sob stories or cajoling from the breeder of the pups. See written proof of the dog's age. WALK AWAY if you are not convinced.

- Rearing
  Critical

How has this puppy been reared so far? In a shed? in the house? Some dogs will manage to overcome a poor start in life because of the resilience of their personality. Sadly, many never fully recover from a poor start.

Family pet puppies should be reared inside the house - in the busiest part of the house. They should have an enriched environment with lots of different things to interact with - boxes, balls, sounds, dangling toys, tunnels ... A thoughtful breeder will have the future mental health of her pups in the front of her mind. Such puppies will have been given the best chance to grow up with no fear and anxiety problems rearing their ugly heads later on.

- Price
  Irrelevant

The "running costs" of the dog will very quickly overtake any significance in the cost price. I tend to forget to ask the price till I've chosen the puppy. Proper, caring breeders are not looking to fleece you.

Be aware, though, that those unscrupulous puppy farmers can charge ridiculous sums of money for a very poor specimen of doubtful parentage which happens to be in fashion. *Caveat emptor!*

Where should I get my puppy from?

Once you've got an idea what type, size, sex, and age of dog you're looking for, now you can source your puppy.

- Breeder
  Super critical!

- *Breed specialist*

There are some fantastic breeders, dedicated to the improvement of their breed, and fanatical about rearing the best puppies possible. They invest a lot of money in genetic testing to ensure their puppies do not suffer from inherited problems (e.g. Hip Dysplasia, Eye diseases, temperament issues - you need to research how these may affect your chosen breed). They devote three months of their life to each litter. They really earn their money! They will give you a detailed puppy pack, with pedigree, registration forms, medical history, diet history, breed-specific advice, and so on. This caring breeder will be interviewing you as a prospective owner when you contact them.

- *Pet dog owner*

Then there are those who have a pet dog who has pups. If there is enough hybrid vigour in the mix you may get away with the absence of genetic testing, as long as the puppies are reared right. These puppies are often reared in the home with lots of love and attention from family and friends, so can be a good bet temperamentally. This would be the old-fashioned household mongrel dog, now sadly disappearing through over-zealous neutering programs. You may be taking pot-luck on size, type, and health.

- *Greeders*

Sadly there are many who I refer to as "greeders". Their interest is in getting as much as possible out of you for as little investment of time and money as possible. They often focus on the most popular breed of the time - currently the physically-troubled brachycephalic breeds like Pugs and French Bulldogs - or the fashionable "designer crossbreeds". Greeders usually focus on small dogs, as they can pack more into their sheds and they cost less to feed.

They may try and offload the puppies at 6 weeks for some spurious reason (the real reason is laziness - this is the most labour-intensive stage of puppy-rearing). No genetic testing is usually done. In my experience it's not uncommon for dogs from these greeders to develop chronic conditions like Hip Dysplasia within their first six months of life, necessitating lifelong medication or surgery. This suffering is appalling when it could so easily have been avoided. These people couldn't care less.

- *Puppy farms/Puppy mills*

The worst of these greeders are the puppy farms aka puppy mills, who have lots of tricks to fool you into buying something that was reared in a filthy cage in a cellar or shed, with no human contact. The poor, overbred bitches and stud dogs live a life of loneliness and misery till they're thrown out as spent.

Often these puppies are much older than is claimed. They even charge a lot of money for them! You'll soon be paying much, much, more for behavioural and veterinary help to try to partially repair the damage these monsters have inflicted. A disproportionate number of dogs bought off the internet classified listings die within their first year. You should not even be looking at these listings.

Do NOT feel sorry for the puppy and take it, even knowing or suspecting its background. You will pay for this rash emotional decision for the whole of the dog's life. Worse, you are giving money to help further this cruel trade. Report the place to the relevant authorities. You can play your part in putting a stop to this dark side of puppy-breeding.

As one otherwise intelligent businesswoman said to me, as she regarded her puppy who had clunky hips, wonky teeth, and was afraid of his own shadow, "I can't believe I fell for those tricks".

You'll find advice about all this through your national kennel club. Many kennel clubs have a breeder assessment scheme.

Meeting your prospective puppy

- Your first viewing
  Very important

When you first visit a litter, do NOT take the family with you. You'd be better taking a friend who hates dogs, who will not be beguiled by the cute little fluffy puppies, and who'll remind you of the priorities you listed as important for you! Decide on those priorities before you go in, and interview the breeder carefully. Ask penetrating questions and require thorough answers with written proofs. A genuine breeder will be interviewing you at the same time, to see if you are a suitable owner for their precious puppies.

The pups should be spotlessly clean and smell sweet, with no tangles or mats, no sticky bum, no runny eyes. Their mother should be interested but not concerned at you handling her pups. (This can be an important pointer to the litter's temperament later on.)

- Buying
  Oh so critical!

On no account agree to a puppy on your first visit. You are looking at a commitment for the next 12-17 years: be fully prepared to WALK AWAY. You know the old saying, "Marry in haste, repent at leisure"!

The ideal puppy is out there waiting for you - make sure you get the right one!

Finally, beware of a breeder who wants you to take a bitch and rear puppies from her - *for them*. It's your choice what you do with your dog. It's not uncommon for a breeder to prevent you being able to register progeny at your national kennel club without their permission. They are trying to protect the health and standards of the breed and protect their puppies from those "greeders".

Choosing YOUR puppy

Your carefully-chosen breeder will help you enormously. She's a fanatic for her breed, usually totally devoted to her own dogs and her own line that she's working hard to improve. She will have spent many hours with this litter of pups. While everyone else thinks they look identical, she'll have given them all nicknames and can tell them apart at a glance. She knows their fads and foibles, their faults and failings. She also knows their best points.

Of course, the breeder of a carefully-reared crossbreed from a much-loved pet in a family home will also know her puppies well and be able to advise.

While you're entitled to see the whole litter together, the breeder will bring out for you the pups that are available - and which she considers suitable for your family and experience.

It's a good idea to visit them twice if possible. The first time they could be half-asleep and dopey and give you a wrong impression. Puppies who appear to be bullying their siblings at 6 weeks will have been taught some manners and bite inhibition by their littermates by the time you see them again at 8 weeks.

Have fun choosing your puppy

I like to play with the puppy and see how interested he is with my toys. I'll bring several different sorts. Interacting with toys at this early age is a good indicator of a strong retrieve later on (great for playing ball on the beach ...) and general teachability.

Unless you are of a shy and retiring disposition yourself, don't feel sorry for the shyest puppy (unless the breeder considers this is the one for you: shyness in a litter is relative!). He could have adjustment problems that you'll have to attempt to work through - and may need professional help.

And all that homework you did? This is the moment of the great pay-off! Because you don't have to consider all those other very important questions any more, you are free to follow your heart.

Spend some time with the puppies the breeder is offering you ... and see which one you fall in love with.

Now you can follow your heart

Just let yourself fall in love. And something surprising might happen ...

When I went to choose Cricket the Whippet, I'd spent almost a year narrowing down the type of whippet I wanted, the breeder (who had the same concerns about breed health as I had), and the mating. The breeder kept me updated with photos and info - first about the dam's pregnancy and whelping, and then about the pups' personalities.

I wanted a bitch. There were three bitches. The breeder was going to choose her favourite for her showing and breeding program, and I had first pick of the other two. I first visited them at 5 weeks.

All three puppies - Poppy, Daisy, and Hannah - were delightful. Poppy outgoing and friendly, Daisy energetic and comical, Hannah sweet and shy.

It was Daisy who "spoke to me". She was the one I really wanted. The breeder had told me she was going to decide between keeping Poppy and Daisy at 7 and a half weeks.

So I told her I'd really like Daisy, but would be perfectly happy with Hannah if Daisy had been chosen by them. The funny thing was that I just didn't relate to Poppy at all. Nothing at all wrong with Poppy, she was a lovely puppy - it just wasn't love at first sight for me.

As it turned out, Poppy was the pup they chose to keep, I got Daisy who became "Cricket", and Hannah went to the delighted third person who had been waiting patiently for us to decide.

Now get this - I had actually wanted a solid colour (same colour all over) which Hannah was, and Daisy was a brindle with white markings. But the heart ruled the head and Cricket is very much loved, adored, and admired.

You just don't know!

But getting all the thorny questions about breeding and health ironed out first gave me complete freedom when I met the pups.

Cricket the Whippet at four months

Or take pot luck

Of course you can choose to disregard this entire chapter and get a puppy found in a cardboard box from your local shelter. This may turn out to be the best puppy ever! All you have to fall back on from here is the advice about the ideal age to get a puppy - stick to that advice!

In this chapter we've learnt

- What sort of puppy to get for our lifestyle
- Where to get it from
- Choosing your individual pup!
- "Are you my new family?"

Conclusion

There's one key point I want you to take away from this book - enjoy your puppy!

Enjoy learning with him. Enjoy watching the wheels turn in his head. Enjoy seeing him try something, think better of it, and try the very thing you want him to do. Enjoy seeing just how intelligent this little fluffball is. Enjoy the fact that you can communicate with another species simply by showing love and patience.

Enjoy the journey - you can worry about the destination another day.

You don't focus on your toddler's future, what exam results she may get, what people will think of her. You enjoy her right now, with jam on her face, shirt on inside out, hair full of sand and leaves from the garden … Parents know that these moments are precious, ephemeral, and elusive.

Enjoy your puppy right now, with mud on his nose, one ear standing up and one floppy, crashed out asleep in the midst of a chewed-up cardboard box. Tomorrow will look after itself. And it will work out perfectly - as long as you enjoy him today.

No blame, no "Nooooo!"

Remember we aren't blaming any*one* or any*thing*. We work with the puppy here before us. What may have gone before is gone. We move forward from where we are.

Yesterday may not have been perfection! But whose "fault" it was is not important. What *is* important is that you learnt the lessons given to you, and know how to be with your pup today, with love and kindness.

Remember that "Nooooo!" gives the puppy no information about what you want her to do - all it tells her is that you're cross, but she has no idea why. Focus instead on what you want, rather than what you don't want. And management is key to ensuring your puppy doesn't do the things you don't want in the first place!

Appropriate and fulsome rewards

Remember that the simplest way to convey what you like to your puppy is to

Reward what you like
Ignore what you don't like
Manage what you can't ignore

This simple mantra will see you happily through most of your life with your dog. Your puppy never does things to annoy you - though he may want attention or a result! - keep in mind that you are on this journey *together*, you are learning *together*.

And never be mean with your affection and treats.

Temper your expectations

We all want to be able to show off our perfect child, well-chosen partner, and well-behaved dog. But Rome wasn't built in a day. Your child's best behaviour may only last a short while before he reverts to being a normal child, you may have kissed a lot of frogs before your prince arrived and went through an adjustment process with you so that you could live happily together.

So allow your puppy to be a puppy! Don't expect perfection when she's so new. Never be tempted to treat her harshly - yanking the lead, talking badly about her, or pushing her about - just to impress someone.

> *There's a splendid old shepherd's saw - that a dog needs a year under each paw before she's any use.*

Once your dog is mature you'll see the benefit of all the work you put in with her. You'll rub along together in comfort and trust. That time will come - right now you're building your future together.

Choice Training

And once you've experienced Choice Training, you won't want to work any other way. With your dog or anyone else. Life becomes so much easier!

Appreciation

I want to offer thanks to all those who have helped me get where I am with my dogs, so that I'm able to help others on the journey:

- First of all, my own long-suffering dogs! They have taught me so much when I've taken the time to listen.
- My students, who have shown me how they learn best, enabling me to give them what they need to know in a way that works for them.
- Some legendary teachers, principal amongst them: Sue Ailsby, Leslie McDevitt, Grisha Stewart, Susan Garrett. I wholeheartedly recommend them. They are trailblazers.

Resources

If you've enjoyed learning about how to start life with your new puppy the right way, and you want to find how to teach all the skills you will need, go to www.brilliantfamilydog.com/books and choose a paperback or ebook for your lap or your reading app. The books are available worldwide through Amazon and all good bookshops (ask the bookshop to order them for you). They're all step-by-step books - I don't leave you hanging!

Calm Down! Step-by-Step to a Calm, Relaxed and Brilliant Family Dog - Book 1

Leave It! How to teach Amazing Impulse Control to your Brilliant Family Dog - Book 2

Let's Go! Enjoy Companionable Walks with your Brilliant Family Dog - Book 3

Here Boy! Step-by-Step to a Stunning Recall from your Brilliant Family Dog - Book 4

or get all four books in one volume in the Essential Skills Boxset

These cover the four skills you need to turn your wild puppy into your Brilliant Family Dog.

For a limited time, you can also get the complete first e-book in this series absolutely free! Go to www.brilliantfamilydog.com/books and you will be reading it in just a few minutes.

Once you've got those Essential Skills under your belt, you can teach your puppy to retrieve, with

Coming soon
Fetch It!
Teach your Brilliant Family Dog to catch, fetch, retrieve, find, and bring things back! - another step-by-step book to have your dog bringing you his toys, your lost car keys, and your slippers. Aaahh.

> I downloaded your books *Calm Down!* and *Leave It!* a few weeks ago and the change in my dog is amazing. He is learning to think about problems and his actions, learning impulse control, and he is so much calmer and happier. He's walking nicely on the lead, he's not stealing food the second I turn my back and we are working on traveling in the car and leaving the house calmly.
> *Anna and Toby*

> I love your books! Your simple, fun, and loving training methods are helping me make tremendous progress with my brilliant puppies.
> *Mary Anne and her two Springer pups*

> I adore your style of training: it works for me and Lola.
> *Pat*

> 5* Amazon review
> My dog is lovely but quite excitable, which made some things really tricky ... The advice in Beverley's books is clear and simple to

follow, and best of all it teaches your dog to think for itself and make good choices without any commands. We now have calm mealtimes, calm leaving the house, a brilliant recall and best of all I have given up using a headcollar, Toby now walks nicely on a loose lead and walks with him have changed from stressful, nagging ordeals into an absolute joy. Seriously, if you want a nicer, better behaved and calmer dog, read these books and follow her steps.

The Brilliant Family dog books are amazing! I have them all.
Adeline

Meanwhile, for more free training, go to www.brilliantfamilydog.com/puppies-and-dogs and get a series of instructional emails on common day-to-day problems like jumping up, chewing, barking, and so on.

Your emails are absolutely wonderful! I love them. Nobody else does anything like this.
Maggie and Archie

The one thing Busta wasn't so good at was greeting people, but since your email we've had everyone popping in to put your tips into place and it worked! Now we no longer have him jumping all over us when we come through the door. Just a very happy dog sat down waggling his tail like mad, waiting for a fuss!
Charlie and Busta

Thank you for sharing your wisdom with us new puppy owners! Although I grew up with dogs and our puppy is our second family dog it doesn't make it any easier!
Sarah

First let me tell you that your housetraining advice was AMAZING. I practiced everything you suggested and within 1-2 days, I had no more accidents in the house. I am thrilled with the practical suggestions, methods and techniques that you have made available on the internet. Your wealth of experience is amazing and your willingness to share it is wonderful. Thank you for what you do.
Elizabeth and Ruby

Hey Beverley, loving being part of your gang!
Sonia and Benson

I am loving your emails and you are covering many issues that I have with my 9 month old Cockerpoo.
Kerry and Meg

COURSES

For more in-depth training - and a wonderful way I can help people all over the world! - check out these two courses which you can find at www.brilliantfamilydog.com/courses:

From Wild Puppy to Brilliant Family Dog (for puppies up to about 9 months)

From Challenging Dog to Brilliant Family Dog (for dogs over 9 months or so)

With over 50 daily videos, an amazingly enthusiastic and supportive private training group, and permanent access, you can join other students from all round the world in changing your relationship with your puppy!

Hello there! Snoopy (our Kelpie puppy) completed this brilliant course with flying colours. The course was amazing and I have highly recommended it to others! We continue to do many of the exercises as just so positive, practical and effective!

Rebecca and Snoopy, student on From Wild Puppy to Brilliant Family Dog

Can't believe how far Echo has come from being terrified of other people, dogs and new sights and experiences. So proud of her. She is listening to me more when we are closer to another person or dog and her recall has been remarked upon by other dog walkers! Our relationship has grown by leaps and bounds doing this course. She has brought so much love and magic to my life and even more so having found your course and books as it has decreased my stress so I'm able to enjoy her more. From wild puppy to engaging companion!

Cluny and Echo, student on From Wild Puppy to Brilliant Family Dog

You will LOVE this course, and one of the many great things about it is you can do it at your own and your dog's pace. No pressure! I am so grateful to Beverley for the knowledge she has given me on how to communicate with my dogs.

Patricia, student on From Challenging Dog to Brilliant Family Dog

Impressive set of dogs you've got and you have been teaching us much! No way I would've have survived without your knowledge - thanks again.

Amal, student on From Challenging Dog to Brilliant Family Dog

If you have a dog who is reactive, anxious or fearful of everything, especially other dogs, you can find lots of resources to help you at www.brilliantfamilydog.com/growly-dogs

And if you've got any specific queries, you can email me direct at beverley@brilliantfamilydog.com This will come straight to my personal inbox and I'll answer you - usually within 48 hours.

Try me!

RESOURCES

Chapter 1
Crate Training
www.youtube.com/watch?v=ebjBo_spqG0

Chapter 2
Children and dog safety
https://doggonesafe.com
stopthe77.com
www.bluecross.org.uk/pet-advice/be-safe-dogs
www.thekennelclub.org.uk/training/safe-and-sound
VIDEO: Lacy plays Retrieve Games
www.brilliantfamilydog.com/retrieve

Chapter 3
Free Socialisation Guide at
https://www.brilliantfamilydog.com/blog/our-familys-always-had-dogs-why-
is-this-one-so-difficult

Chapter 4
Harness
UK www.goodfordogs.co.uk/products *
Worldwide www.2houndsdesign.com

Chapter 5

www.allaboutdogfood.co.uk

www.rawmeatybones.com

For UK readers - three weeks' supply of homecooked food absolutely FREE at
www.butternutbox.com/brilliantfamilydog *

For UK readers - 50% off quality tinned and dry dog food at
www.bobandlush.com/beverleyc *

Chapter 9

www.thekennelclub.org.uk/breeding/assured-breeder-scheme

www.akc.org/breeder-programs/akc-breeder-of-merit-program

www.thekennelclub.org.uk/our-resources/kennel-club-campaigns/puppy-
farming

* If you purchase through these links I will benefit - but you'll benefit more!

For a free list of the Puppy Gear you need, go to
www.brilliantfamilydog.com/blog/puppy-gear-what-do-you-really-need
And download it straight away!

Don't go without your free book!

Get the next piece of the puzzle for your dog

Get the first digital book in the series,
Essential Skills for your Brilliant Family Dog
absolutely free here
https://www.brilliantfamilydog.com/freebook-calm-down

About the Author

I've been training dogs for many years. First for competitive dog sports and over time to be stellar family pets. For most of my life, I've lived with up to four dogs at a time, so I'm well used to getting a multi-dog household to run smoothly. It soon became clear that a force-free approach was by far the most successful, effective, and rewarding for me and the dogs.

I've done the necessary studying for my various qualifications - for rehab of anxious and fearful "aggressive" dogs, early puppy development, and learning theory and its practical applications. I am continually studying and learning this endlessly amazing subject!

There are some superb teachers and advocates of force-free dog training, and you'll find those I am particularly indebted to in the Resources Section. Some of the methods I show you are well-known in the force-free dog training community, while many have my own particular twist.

A lot of my learning has come through the Puppy Classes, Tutored Puppy Walks, and Starter Classes I teach. These dog-owners are not looking for competition-standard training; they just want a Brilliant Family Dog they can take anywhere. More recently I've been able to extend my understanding by interacting with readers of my books, and with students of my busy online courses, and delight in the change they are able to achieve.

Working with real dogs and their real owners keeps me humble - and resourceful! It's no good being brilliant at training dogs if you can't convey this enthusiasm and knowledge to the person the dog has to live with. So I'm grateful for everything my students have taught me about how they learn best.

Beverley Courtney
BA(Hons), CBATI, CAP2, MAPDT(UK), ABTC Registered Animal Instructor